# The Member of the Wedding

## *Also by Carson McCullers*

# The Member
of the Wedding

A PLAY BY
## CARSON McCULLERS

WITH AN INTRODUCTION BY
## DOROTHY ALLISON

## A New Directions Book

to Reeves McCullers

# INTRODUCTION
## by Dorothy Allison

Twelve, twelve and a half, twelve and five-sixths, almost thirteen years old—has anyone ever written about adolescent girls in the particular way that Carson McCullers did?

We look back at *The Member of the Wedding* from a completely different mentality—one remade not only by the changes wrought by the civil rights movement, the women's movement, and the multilayered context of the fight for lesbian and gay freedoms, but by the shifts in how gender and gender perceptions have altered as a result of all these struggles. Many of the most far-reaching changes in how we think about adolescent girls have come from our literature. Inhabiting all these youngsters—from Scout in *To Kill a Mockingbird* to the murdered child in *The Lovely Bones* to the most recent revelation of memoir or biography—we have learned to take for granted what Carson McCullers crafted in *The Member of the Wedding*: an extraordinary and startling revelation of a tormented psyche on the cusp of change. What she so deftly portrayed was nearly unknown and certainly unspoken—an essentially queer girl, bursting with outrage, desire, and naiveté.

"Wait." I can hear you now. "Wait, are you saying that Frankie Adams was a lesbian?"

Yes, she was a lesbian, in the same way that Bone was in my own novel, *Bastard Out of Carolina*—a girl focused on other girls, her friendships with them, and their opinion of her. More to the point, Frankie Adams was *queer*—decidedly out of step with everything she was expected to be and become. She was what we have come to know from so many books since this one was first published—queer in the same way that all smart, miserable, rebellious, almost-teenage girls are when they do not want to become the women the world wants them to become. It was Carson McCullers' gift to render girls so complex and almost unbearably raw and vibrant that we understand immediately how it is to be driven manic by our own hopes and dreams, and fears.

Will Frankie grow up to be as focused and hungry for the close attention and deep friendship of another girl as she is in this story? That I do not know. Girls at adolescence are neither finished nor fated. In a safe and open-ended reality, they might become anything. In the world as it is, and especially as it was in the 1940s, the possibilities are much more limited, much less hopeful. It seems to me that Frankie may very well grow up as Carson did—to marry a man as uncomfortable with what the world wanted him to be as she was; and in the same way Frankie may grow to distrust love, and the demands and expectations of the beloved, as well as to inhabit, as Carson did, a life shaped by passionate, intimate, but rarely fulfilled obsessions with women who would never see her as the beloved.

The grown up version of Frankie might have become terribly unhappy, but she may also have become stubbornly passionately hopeful, and turned her disappointment and insight to the creation of works of genius as deeply felt as any we have since been given. Or she might have simply run away from home and died drunk on despair. I am a novelist, a lesbian, and as much a romantic obsessive as Carson herself, and I can imagine all these possibilities.

What Carson McCullers achieved in her creation of Frankie Adams and *The Member of the Wedding*, was more than a diatribe against gender oppression or the injustice of bending so perverse an imagination to the rigid constraints demanded of the "good girl" in the 1940s American South. Oh yes, there is much to understand and reflect on from the queer content of the play, but there is just as much to understand about the artist, the loner, the Southerner, the passionate advocate of justice and human possibility. We still have much to learn from the woman who could create as nuanced and insightful a character as Berenice who, in the novella, dreams of a world in which there was "no war . . . No stiff corpses hanging from the Europe trees and no Jews murdered anywhere. No killed Jews and no hurt colored people. No war and no hunger in the world." Yes, there is much to be learned from the creator of Frankie, whose vision of paradise includes war: at least to the extent that she can imagine she will "dress up like a boy and join the Merchant Marines and run away to sea." Frankie knows her own ambitions and desires.

Arguing and imagining, these two pull us into a reality in which a twelve-and-five-sixths-year-old white girl and a black woman (hired to cook and watch over her) take each other and the questions about responsibility, happiness, and justice completely seriously. By the time we are introduced to the leavening influence of John Henry and his six-year-old's paradise, we are ready to do as he does, to close our eyes and smile. He asks, "How did that boy change into a girl? Did he kiss his elbow?" He bends to kiss his own elbow in homage to the act, and it is John Henry we want to kiss—to make magic and will him to live forever. He is so easy with himself and these two extraordinary women. He takes no offense when Frankie yells at him to go away, that she is sick of him. Her moods do not threaten him. He dreams aloud of the pin-headed girl in the freak pavilion, the one they saw at the fair. "She was," he says, "the cutest little girl I ever saw. I never saw anything so cute in my whole life, did you, Frankie?"

But Frankie is appalled. That girl from the freak pavilion with her head no bigger than an orange had her "hair shaved off and a big pink bow at the top." It does not take much for us to see the connection—convinced that she is freakish tall, her own hair cut short and a ribbon tied about her head,

Frankie will try to stretch her hair a bit longer for the wedding. Frankie fears her own freak nature, her own queer insides. She has lost the grace that lets John Henry see the marvelous in the strange, she needs Berenice to reassure her that she will not grow into a freak herself.

"Do you think I will be pretty?"

"Maybe, if you file down them horns a bit."

We are in no freak pavilion, we are in human company with the desperate, the uncertain and those graced by the ability to kiss their own elbows and wish themselves something else again.

This Frankie, grown too tall, too fast, with her hair cropped ragged and short, all sweat-streaked and garbed in t-shirt and shorts—she knows the oddity she presents. This Frankie is terrified and desperate not to be so. She is not so much in love with her brother and his bride as she is with the loved couple they make—the joined and free beings she idealizes and wants to become. They are not only beautiful and happy, but open to the whole wide world into which Frankie too wants to step, and from which she fears she will forever be denied access. How can she be free? She is a non-member, an unjoined person who wants to be what she is not—safe, joined, at one with the beautiful and the blessed.

That essential desire defines for me what it means to be twelve, almost thirteen years old. This is the age at which we most want to be one with our own—our tribe, our family, our nation. This is when we feel ourselves so painfully denied and isolated in our excruciatingly self-conscious bodies, even if we are the most normal-seeming young person in the neighborhood. No one feels normal at thirteen, no one feels acceptable. We are uncomfortable in our own skin, peering into our mirrors anxiously; certain no one else feels what we feel. Most terribly, we ache with the fear that we will never find our place or our people, that we will never fit in or be one with anyone, never be accepted, and never escape the stinging nettles of our own nervous system. We will be members of nothing, joined to no one, always alone.

Is there anything more terrifying, particularly at not quite thirteen?

The response to this intensity is not only despair (have you looked at teenagers lately?), but rage. That rage, and the accompanying outrage, is justified.

The raging despairing Frankie brandishing that knife and running circles around the kitchen is scary wonderful. Caught in the close embrace of Berenice and pulled bodily back into a moment of calm, she near breaks our hearts. Then sandwiched between Berenice and that charmed and charming John Henry, she achieves an almost mythic power—an image of love and acceptance that does not deny its core of grief and anger.

We have grown used to this girl in the years since Carson first put her on the stage, at least in some measure. We have grown able to look at her and see past the vibrating intensity to other girls, some less desperate, but no less caught in that moment between explosion and acceptance. We forget what a shock it must have been to meet her in the novella in 1946, or when Julie Harris first burst onto the stage as Frankie in 1950. We forget Frankie as she was, hinting at acts and understandings that have become commonplace in our modern world—sexual touches and desires delicately nuanced in this play (and as delicately rendered) as Frankie's confused and uncertain memories of things she has done or pretended not to have done. Her genuine confusion and outrage at any mention of sex, the "nasty lies"—can we imagine it in a teenage girl of today? What in 2006 we may jump past, was originally rendered with the most subtle, suggestive touches by a mind that had never seen television or read a graphic novel. Nothing was denied or hidden, except what Frankie could not imagine or put into words for herself. But that is a world in some ways more dangerous and hurtful than the one we can speak about so freely these days. The list of the unspoken and the unspeakable hovers over every word and gesture young Frankie makes. The things she cannot see, we think we can—though there are days I am not sure our vision is any more perceptive than hers.

Frankie was a child of her time, becoming a woman, a particular kind of woman, capable of insight and compassion and with a deep-seated sense of justice and outrage, but one just as capable of retreat, of squeezing herself down into as small a kernel as might seem safe to one so full of need and terror. The girl we meet in the beginning of the play is not the one who walks out the door at its end—and the tragedy of this truth is undiminished by all the decades that have passed since Carson McCullers made her.

The contemporary tragedy of *The Member of the Wedding* is how invisible Frankie has become in the years since she was made, how rarely she has been read. We forget her in full when we see her only in snatches, quotes lifted from the text, commentary, criticism, and reflection. Not reading her in full, we mistake her, and lose her—and with her the author, the magician who mined her own soul in this creation.

Talking about Carson McCullers to people who have not read *The Member of the Wedding*, or *The Heart is a Lonely Hunter*, or *Reflections in a Golden Eye*, or *The Ballad of the Sad Café* is like discussing recipes with people who have never eaten the food you love most. A conversation is possible, but one of us is just repeating or responding to what we have heard. Denatured, empty, prejudged and maddening conversations like this take place all the time because so few people have recently read her work. They talk philosophically, or reflect from memory, without the insight and passion you get from reading the original.

Talking about the writing, about adolescence, or about the legend of Carson McCullers herself (how she always looked a kind of adolescent even as a grown woman), about other famous writers of the period, her contemporaries and friends who advocated for her genius or bemoaned her poor choices, or even talking about how she was misunderstood or disdained for all the usual reasons (being female, Southern, romantic, and preternaturally feminist before there was a feminist movement)—all that is enthralling and interesting and far too easy. To talk about Carson McCullers without rereading the books and addressing what she made on the page is simply outrageous. (Frankie would take up her knife and pick her scabs in despair.)

Take up these pages and let yourself fall into them. Let Carson McCullers catch you—her people, her language, and yes, this intricately rendered, almost architectural play; three main characters, three acts, and the tripled internal resonance. Notice the word choices, the repetitions, and the pacing. Surprise yourself with the genius of the layers, the reflections, and the way everything starts at a high pitch and slowly paces down like an overheated girl gradually cooling, lifting her head, and looking around. Measure the choices she makes against what we know of that time and the world she inhabits. This twelve, not quite thirteen, year-old ages a world in a few days, revealing everything there is to see in the process of becoming a member, a ready-to-be-joined person.

This is not a small work, this is a great one.

Read it again, every little while. Then lift your head and look around. Measure what has changed, and what has not. It is, every time, a revelation.

February 2006

# CHARACTERS

BERENICE SADIE BROWN

FRANKIE ADDAMS

JOHN HENRY WEST

JARVIS

JANICE

MR. ADDAMS

MRS. WEST

HELEN FLETCHER

DORIS

SIS LAURA

T. T. WILLIAMS

HONEY CAMDEN BROWN

BARNEY MacKEAN

TIME: *August, 1945*

PLACE: *A small Southern town*

ACT ONE        A late afternoon in August

ACT TWO        Afternoon of the next day

ACT THREE
  *Scene One*        The wedding day—afternoon of the
                          next day following Act Two

  *Scene Two*        4 A.M. the following morning

  *Scene Three*        Late afternoon, in the following
                          November

*The Member of the Wedding* was first produced in New York on January 5, 1950 at the Empire Theater by Robert Whitehead, Oliver Rea and Stanley Martineau. The play was directed by Harold Clurman, with sets designed by Lester Polakov. The opening cast was as follows:

| | |
|---|---|
| BERENICE SADIE BROWN | Ethel Waters |
| FRANKIE ADDAMS | Julie Harris |
| JOHN HENRY WEST | Brandon de Wilde |
| JARVIS | James Holden |
| JANICE | Janet de Gore |
| MR. ADDAMS | William Hansen |
| MRS. WEST | Margaret Barker |
| HELEN FLETCHER | Mitzie Blake |
| DORIS | Joan Shepard |
| SIS LAURA | Phyliss Walker |
| T. T. WILLIAMS | Harry Bolden |
| HONEY CAMDEN BROWN | Henry Scott |
| BARNEY MACKEAN | Jimmy Dutton |

# ACT ONE

# ACT ONE

*A part of a Southern back yard and kitchen. At stage left there is a scuppernong arbor. A sheet, used as a stage curtain, hangs raggedly at one side of the arbor. There is an elm tree in the yard. The kitchen has in the center a table with chairs. The walls are drawn with child drawings. There is a stove to the right and a small coal heating stove with coal scuttle in rear center of kitchen. The kitchen opens on the left into the yard. At the interior right a door leads to a small inner room. A door at the left leads into the front hall. The lights go on dimly, with a dream-like effect, gradually revealing the family in the yard and Berenice Sadie Brown in the kitchen. Berenice, the cook, is a stout, motherly Negro woman with an air of great capability and devoted protection. She is about forty-five years old. She has a quiet, flat face and one of her eyes is made of blue glass. Sometimes, when her socket bothers her, she dispenses with the false eye and wears a black patch. When we first see her she is wearing the patch and is dressed in a simple print work dress and apron.*

*Frankie, a gangling girl of twelve with blonde hair cut like a boy's, is wearing shorts and a sombrero and is standing in the arbor gazing adoringly at her brother Jarvis and his fiancée Janice. She is a dreamy, restless girl, and periods of energetic activity alternate with a rapt attention to her inward world of fantasy. She is thin and awkward and very much aware of being too tall. Jarvis, a good-looking boy of twenty-one, wearing an army uniform, stands by Janice. He is awkward when he first appears because this is his betrothal visit. Janice, a young, pretty, fresh-looking girl of eighteen or nineteen is charming but rather ordinary, with brown hair done up in a small knot. She is dressed in her best clothes and is anxious to be liked by*

1

*her new family. Mr. Addams, Frankie's father, is a deliberate and absent-minded man of about forty-five. A widower of many years, he has become set in his habits. He is dressed conservatively, and there is about him an old-fashioned look and manner. John Henry, Frankie's small cousin, aged seven, picks and eats any scuppernongs he can reach. He is a delicate, active boy and wears gold-rimmed spectacles which give him an oddly judicious look. He is blond and sunburned and when we first see him he is wearing a sun-suit and is barefooted.*

[*Berenice Sadie Brown is busy in the kitchen.*]

JARVIS:

Seems to me like this old arbor has shrunk. I remember when I was a child it used to seem absolutely enormous. When I was Frankie's age, I had a vine swing here. Remember, Papa?

FRANKIE:

It don't seem so absolutely enormous to me, because I am so tall.

JARVIS:

I never saw a human grow so fast in all my life. I think maybe we ought to tie a brick to your head.

FRANKIE [*hunching down in obvious distress*]:
Oh, Jarvis! Don't.

JANICE:

Don't tease your little sister. I don't think Frankie is too tall. She probably won't grow much more. I had the biggest portion of my growth by the time I was thirteen.

2

FRANKIE:

But I'm just twelve. When I think of all the growing years ahead of me, I get scared.

[*Janice goes to Frankie and puts her arms around her comfortingly. Frankie stands rigid, embarrassed and blissful.*]

JANICE:

I wouldn't worry.

[*Berenice comes from the kitchen with a tray of drinks. Frankie rushes eagerly to help her serve them.*]

FRANKIE:

Let me help.

BERENICE:

Them two drinks is lemonade for you and John Henry. The others got liquor in them.

FRANKIE:

Janice, come sit on the arbor seat. Jarvis, you sit down too.

[*Jarvis and Janice sit close together on the wicker bench in the arbor. Frankie hands the drinks around, then perches on the ground before Janice and Jarvis and stares adoringly at them.*]

FRANKIE:

It was such a surprise when Jarvis wrote home you are going to be married.

JANICE:

I hope it wasn't a bad surprise.

3

FRANKIE:

Oh, Heavens no! [*with great feeling*] As a matter of fact . . . [*She strokes Janice's shoes tenderly and Jarvis' army boot.*] If only you knew how I feel.

MR. ADDAMS:

Frankie's been bending my ears ever since your letter came, Jarvis. Going on about weddings, brides, grooms, etc.

JANICE:

It's lovely that we can be married at Jarvis' home.

MR. ADDAMS:

That's the way to feel, Janice. Marriage is a sacred institution.

FRANKIE:

Oh, it will be beautiful.

JARVIS:

Pretty soon we'd better be shoving off for Winter Hill. I have to be back in barracks tonight.

FRANKIE:

Winter Hill is such a lovely, cold name. It reminds me of ice and snow.

JANICE:

You know it's just a hundred miles away, darling.

JARVIS:

Ice and snow indeed! Yesterday the temperature on the parade ground reached 102.

4

[*Frankie takes a palmetto fan from the table and fans first Janice, then Jarvis.*]

JANICE:
That feels so good, darling. Thanks.

FRANKIE:
I wrote you so many letters, Jarvis, and you never, never would answer me. When you were stationed in Alaska, I wanted so much to hear about Alaska. I sent you so many boxes of home-made candy, but you never answered me.

JARVIS:
Oh, Frankie. You know how it is . . .

FRANKIE [*sipping her drink*]:
You know this lemonade tastes funny. Kind of sharp and hot. I believe I got the drinks mixed up.

JARVIS:
I was thinking my drink tasted mighty sissy. Just plain lemonade—no liquor at all.

[*Frankie and Jarvis exchange their drinks. Jarvis sips his.*]

JARVIS:
This is better.

FRANKIE:
I drank a lot. I wonder if I'm drunk. It makes me feel like I had four legs instead of two. I think I'm drunk. [*She gets up and begins to stagger around in imitation of drunkenness.*] See! I'm drunk! Look, Papa, how drunk I am! [*Sud-*

5

*denly she turns a handspring; then there is a blare of music from the club house gramophone off to the right.*]

JANICE:
Where does the music come from? It sounds so close.

FRANKIE:
It is. Right over there. They have club meetings and parties with boys on Friday nights. I watch them here from the yard.

JANICE:
It must be nice having your club house so near.

FRANKIE:
I'm not a member now. But they are holding an election this afternoon, and maybe I'll be elected.

JOHN HENRY:
Here comes Mama.

[*Mrs. West, John Henry's mother, crosses the yard from the right. She is a vivacious, blonde woman of about thirty-three. She is dressed in sleazy, rather dowdy summer clothes.*]

MR. ADDAMS:
Hello, Pet. Just in time to meet our new family member.

MRS. WEST:
I saw you out here from the window.

JARVIS [*rising, with Janice*]:
Hi, Aunt Pet. How is Uncle Eustace?

6

MRS. WEST:
He's at the office.

JANICE [*offering her hand with the engagement ring on it*]:
Look, Aunt Pet. May I call you Aunt Pet?

MRS. WEST [*hugging her*]:
Of course, Janice. What a gorgeous ring!

JANICE:
Jarvis just gave it to me this morning. He wanted to consult his father and get it from his store, naturally.

MRS. WEST:
How lovely.

MR. ADDAMS:
A quarter carat—not too flashy but a good stone.

MRS. WEST [*to Berenice, who is gathering up the empty glasses*]:
Berenice, what have you and Frankie been doing to my John Henry? He sticks over here in your kitchen morning, noon and night.

BERENICE:
We enjoys him and Candy seems to like it over here.

MRS. WEST:
What on earth do you do to him?

BERENICE:
We just talks and passes the time of day. Occasionally plays cards.

MRS. WEST:
Well, if he gets in your way just shoo him home.

BERENICE:
Candy don't bother nobody.

JOHN HENRY [*walking around barefooted in the arbor*]:
These grapes are so squelchy when I step on them.

MRS. WEST:
Run home, darling, and wash your feet and put on your sandals.

JOHN HENRY:
I like to squelch on the grapes.

[*Berenice goes back to the kitchen.*]

JANICE:
That looks like a stage curtain. Jarvis told me how you used to write plays and act in them out here in the arbor. What kind of shows do you have?

FRANKIE:
Oh, crook shows and cowboy shows. This summer I've had some cold shows—about Esquimos and explorers—on account of the hot weather.

JANICE:
Do you ever have romances?

FRANKIE:
Naw . . . [*with bravado*] I had crook shows for the most part. You see I never believed in love until now. [*Her look*

*lingers on Janice and Jarvis. She hugs Janice and Jarvis, bending over them from back of the bench.*]

MRS. WEST:
Frankie and this little friend of hers gave a performance of "The Vagabond King" out here last spring.

[*John Henry spreads out his arms and imitates the heroine of the play from memory, singing in his high childish voice.*]

JOHN HENRY:
Never hope to bind me. Never hope to know. [*speaking*] Frankie was the king-boy. I sold the tickets.

MRS. WEST:
Yes, I have always said that Frankie has talent.

FRANKIE:
Aw, I'm afraid I don't have much talent.

JOHN HENRY:
Frankie can laugh and kill people good. She can die, too.

FRANKIE [*with some pride*]:
Yeah, I guess I die all right.

MR. ADDAMS:
Frankie rounds up John Henry and those smaller children, but by the time she dresses them in the costumes, they're worn out and won't act in the show.

JARVIS [*looking at his watch*]:
Well, it's time we shove off for Winter Hill—Frankie's

9

land of icebergs and snow—where the temperature goes up to 102.

[*Jarvis takes Janice's hand. He gets up and gazes fondly around the yard and the arbor. He pulls her up and stands with his arm around her, gazing around him at the arbor and yard.*]

JARVIS:
It carries me back—this smell of mashed grapes and dust. I remember all the endless summer afternoons of my childhood. It does carry me back.

FRANKIE:
Me too. It carries me back, too.

MR. ADDAMS [*putting one arm around Janice and shaking Jarvis' hand*]:
Merciful Heavens! It seems I have two Methuselahs in my family! Does it carry you back to your childhood too, John Henry?

JOHN HENRY:
Yes, Uncle Royal.

MR. ADDAMS:
Son, this visit was a real pleasure. Janice, I'm mighty pleased to see my boy has such lucky judgment in choosing a wife.

FRANKIE:
I hate to think you have to go. I'm just now realizing you're here.

JARVIS:

We'll be back in two days. The wedding is Sunday.

[*The family move around the house toward the street. John Henry enters the kitchen through the back door. There are the sounds of "good-byes" from the front yard.*]

JOHN HENRY:

Frankie was drunk. She drank a liquor drink.

BERENICE:

She just made out like she was drunk—pretended.

JOHN HENRY:

She said, "Look, Papa, how drunk I am," and she couldn't walk.

FRANKIE'S VOICE:

Good-bye, Jarvis. Good-bye, Janice.

JARVIS' VOICE:

See you Sunday.

MR. ADDAMS' VOICE:

Drive carefully, son. Good-bye, Janice.

JANICE'S VOICE:

Good-bye and thanks, Mr. Addams. Good-bye, Frankie darling.

ALL THE VOICES:

Good-bye! Good-bye!

JOHN HENRY:

They are going now to Winter Hill.

11

[*There is the sound of the front door opening, then of steps in the hall. Frankie enters through the hall.*]

FRANKIE:
Oh, I can't understand it! The way it all just suddenly happened.

BERENICE:
Happened? Happened?

FRANKIE:
I have never been so puzzled.

BERENICE:
Puzzled about what?

FRANKIE:
The whole thing. They are so beautiful.

BERENICE [*after a pause*]:
I believe the sun done fried your brains.

JOHN HENRY [*whispering*]:
Me too.

BERENICE:
Look here at me. You jealous.

FRANKIE:
Jealous?

BERENICE:
Jealous because your brother's going to be married.

FRANKIE [*slowly*]:
No. I just never saw any two people like them. When they walked in the house today it was so queer.

BERENICE:
You jealous. Go and behold yourself in the mirror. I can see from the color of your eyes.

[*Frankie goes to the mirror and stares. She draws up her left shoulder, shakes her head, and turns away.*]

FRANKIE [*with feeling*]:
Oh! They were the two prettiest people I ever saw. I just can't understand how it happened.

BERENICE:
Whatever ails you?—actin' so queer.

FRANKIE:
I don't know. I bet they have a good time every minute of the day.

JOHN HENRY:
Less us have a good time.

FRANKIE:
Us have a good time? Us? [*She rises and walks around the table.*]

BERENICE:
Come on. Less have a game of three-handed bridge.

[*They sit down to the table, shuffle the cards, deal, and play a game.*]

13

FRANKIE:
Oregon, Alaska, Winter Hill, the wedding. It's all so queer.

BERENICE:
I can't bid, never have a hand these days.

FRANKIE:
A spade.

JOHN HENRY:
I want to bid spades. That's what I was going to bid.

FRANKIE:
Well, that's your tough luck. I bid them first.

JOHN HENRY:
Oh, you fool jackass! It's not fair!

BERENICE:
Hush quarreling, you two. [*She looks at both their hands.*]
To tell the truth, I don't think either of you got such a
grand hand to fight over the bid about. Where is the
cards? I haven't had no kind of a hand all week.

FRANKIE:
I don't give a durn about it. It is immaterial with me.
[*There is a long pause. She sits with her head propped on
her hand, her legs wound around each other.*] Let's talk
about them—and the wedding.

BERENICE:
What you want to talk about?

FRANKIE:

My heart feels them going away—going farther and farther away—while I am stuck here by myself.

BERENICE:

You ain't here by yourself. By the way, where's your Pa?

FRANKIE:

He went to the store. I think about them, but I remembered them more as a feeling than as a picture.

BERENICE:

A feeling?

FRANKIE:

They were the two prettiest people I ever saw. Yet it was like I couldn't see all of them I wanted to see. My brains couldn't gather together quick enough to take it all in. And then they were gone.

BERENICE:

Well, stop commenting about it. You don't have your mind on the game.

FRANKIE [*playing her cards, followed by John Henry*]:
Spades are trumps and you got a spade. I have some of my mind on the game.

[*John Henry puts his donkey necklace in his mouth and looks away.*]

FRANKIE:

Go on, cheater.

BERENICE:

Make haste.

JOHN HENRY:

I can't. It's a king. The only spade I got is a king, and I don't want to play my king under Frankie's ace. And I'm not going to do it either.

FRANKIE [*throwing her cards down on the table*]:
See, Berenice, he cheats!

BERENICE:

Play your king, John Henry. You have to follow the rules of the game.

JOHN HENRY:
My king. It isn't fair.

FRANKIE:
Even with this trick, I can't win.

BERENICE:

Where is the cards? For three days I haven't had a decent hand. I'm beginning to suspicion something. Come on less us count these old cards.

FRANKIE:

We've worn these old cards out. If you would eat these old cards, they would taste like a combination of all the dinners of this summer together with a sweaty-handed, nasty taste. Why, the jacks and the queens are missing.

BERENICE:

John Henry, how come you do a thing like that? So that's why you asked for the scissors and stole off quiet behind the arbor. Now Candy, how come you took our playing cards and cut out the pictures?

JOHN HENRY:
Because I wanted them. They're cute.

FRANKIE:
See? He's nothing but a child. It's hopeless. Hopeless!

BERENICE:
Maybe so.

FRANKIE:
We'll just have to put him out of the game. He's entirely too young.

[*John Henry whimpers.*]

BERENICE:
Well, we can't put Candy out of the game. We gotta have a third to play. Besides, by the last count he owes me close to three million dollars.

FRANKIE:
Oh, I am sick unto death. [*She sweeps the cards from the table, then gets up and begins walking around the kitchen. John Henry leaves the table and picks up a large blonde doll on the chair in the corner.*] I wish they'd taken me with them to Winter Hill this afternoon. I wish tomorrow was Sunday instead of Saturday.

BERENICE:
Sunday will come.

FRANKIE:
I doubt it. I wish I was going somewhere for good. I wish I had a hundred dollars and could just light out and never see this town again.

17

BERENICE:
It seems like you wish for a lot of things.

FRANKIE:
I wish I was somebody else except me.

JOHN HENRY [*holding the doll*]:
You serious when you gave me the doll a while ago?

FRANKIE:
It gives me a pain just to think about them.

BERENICE:
It is a known truth that gray-eyed peoples are jealous.

[*There are sounds of children playing in the neighboring yard.*]

JOHN HENRY:
Let's go out and play with the children.

FRANKIE:
I don't want to.

JOHN HENRY:
There's a big crowd, and they sound like they having a mighty good time. Less go.

FRANKIE:
You got ears. You heard me.

JOHN HENRY:
I think maybe I better go home.

18

FRANKIE:

Why, you said you were going to spend the night. You just can't eat dinner and then go off in the afternoon like that.

JOHN HENRY:

I know it.

BERENICE:

Candy, Lamb, you can go home if you want to.

JOHN HENRY:

But less go out, Frankie. They sound like they having a lot of fun.

FRANKIE:

No, they're not. Just a crowd of ugly, silly children. Running and hollering and running and hollering. Nothing to it.

JOHN HENRY:

Less go!

FRANKIE:

Well, then I'll entertain you. What do you want to do? Would you like for me to read to you out of The Book of Knowledge, or would you rather do something else?

JOHN HENRY:

I rather do something else. [*He goes to the back door, and looks into the yard. Several young girls of thirteen or fourteen, dressed in clean print frocks, file slowly across the back yard.*] Look. Those big girls.

FRANKIE [*running out into the yard*]:

Hey, there. I'm mighty glad to see you. Come on in.

19

HELEN:

We can't. We were just passing through to notify our new member.

FRANKIE [*overjoyed*]:

Am I the new member?

DORIS:

No, you're not the one the club elected.

FRANKIE:

Not elected?

HELEN:

Every ballot was unanimous for Mary Littlejohn.

FRANKIE:

Mary Littlejohn! You mean that girl who just moved in next door? That pasty fat girl with those tacky pigtails? The one who plays the piano all day long?

DORIS:

Yes. The club unanimously elected Mary.

FRANKIE:

Why, she's not even cute.

HELEN:

She is too; and, furthermore, she's talented.

FRANKIE:

I think it's sissy to sit around the house all day playing classical music.

DORIS:

Why, Mary is training for a concert career.

FRANKIE:

Well, I wish to Jesus she would train somewhere else.

DORIS:

You don't have enough sense to appreciate a talented girl like Mary.

FRANKIE:

What are you doing in my yard? You're never to set foot on my Papa's property again. [*Frankie shakes Helen.*] Son-of-a-bitches. I could shoot you with my Papa's pistol.

JOHN HENRY [*shaking his fists*]:

Son-of-a-bitches.

FRANKIE:

Why didn't you elect me? [*She goes back into the house.*] Why can't I be a member?

JOHN HENRY:

Maybe they'll change their mind and invite you.

BERENICE:

I wouldn't pay them no mind. All my life I've been wantin' things that I ain't been gettin'. Anyhow those club girls is fully two years older than you.

FRANKIE:

I think they have been spreading it all over town that I smell bad. When I had those boils and had to use that black bitter-smelling ointment, old Helen Fletcher asked me what was that funny smell I had. Oh, I could shoot every one of them with a pistol.

*[Frankie sits with her head on the table. John Henry approaches and pats the back of Frankie's neck.]*

JOHN HENRY:

I don't think you smell so bad. You smell sweet, like a hundred flowers.

FRANKIE:

The son-of-a-bitches. And there was something else. They were telling nasty lies about married people. When I think of Aunt Pet and Uncle Eustace! And my own father! The nasty lies! I don't know what kind of fool they take me for.

BERENICE:

That's what I tell you. They too old for you.

*[John Henry raises his head, expands his nostrils and sniffs at himself. Then Frankie goes into the interior bedroom and returns with a bottle of perfume.]*

FRANKIE:

Boy! I bet I use more perfume than anybody else in town. Want some on you, John Henry? You want some, Berenice? [She sprinkles perfume.]

JOHN HENRY:

Like a thousand flowers.

BERENICE:

Frankie, the whole idea of a club is that there are members who are included and the non-members who are not included. Now what you ought to do is to round you up a club of your own. And you could be the president yourself. [There is a pause.]

FRANKIE:

Who would I get?

BERENICE:

Why, those little children you hear playing in the neighborhood.

FRANKIE:

I don't want to be the president of all those little young left-over people.

BERENICE:

Well, then enjoy your misery. That perfume smells so strong it kind of makes me sick.

[*John Henry plays with the doll at the kitchen table and Frankie watches.*]

FRANKIE:

Look here at me, John Henry. Take off those glasses. [*John Henry takes off his glasses.*] I bet you don't need those glasses. [*She points to the coal scuttle.*] What is this?

JOHN HENRY:

The coal scuttle.

FRANKIE [*taking a shell from the kitchen shelf*]:

And this?

JOHN HENRY:

The shell we got at Saint Peter's Bay last summer.

FRANKIE:

What is that little thing crawling around on the floor?

23

JOHN HENRY:
Where?

FRANKIE:
That little thing crawling around near your feet.

JOHN HENRY:
Oh. [*He squats down.*] Why, it's an ant. How did that get in here?

FRANKIE:
If I were you I'd just throw those glasses away. You can see good as anybody.

BERENICE:
Now quit picking with John Henry.

FRANKIE:
They don't look becoming. [*John Henry wipes his glasses and puts them back on.*] He can suit himself. I was only telling him for his own good. [*She walks restlessly around the kitchen.*] I bet Janice and Jarvis are members of a lot of clubs. In fact, the army is kind of like a club.

[*John Henry searches through Berenice's pocketbook.*]

BERENICE:
Don't root through my pocketbook like that, Candy. Ain't a wise policy to search folks' pocketbooks. They might think you trying to steal their money.

JOHN HENRY:
I'm looking for your new glass eye. Here it is. [*He hands Berenice the glass eye.*] You got two nickels and a dime.

24

[*Berenice takes off her patch, turns away and inserts the glass eye.*]

BERENICE:

I ain't used to it yet. The socket bothers me. Maybe it don't fit properly.

JOHN HENRY:

The blue glass eye looks very cute.

FRANKIE:

I don't see why you had to get that eye. It has a wrong expression—let alone being blue.

BERENICE:

Ain't anybody ask your judgment, wise-mouth.

JOHN HENRY:

Which one of your eyes do you see out of the best?

BERENICE:

The left eye, of course. The glass eye don't do me no seeing good at all.

JOHN HENRY:

I like the glass eye better. It is so bright and shiny—a real pretty eye. Frankie, you serious when you gave me this doll a while ago?

FRANKIE:

Janice and Jarvis. It gives me this pain just to think about them.

BERENICE:

It is a known truth that gray-eyed people are jealous.

25

FRANKIE:
I told you I wasn't jealous. I couldn't be jealous of one of them without being jealous of them both. I 'sociate the two of them together. Somehow they're just so different from us.

BERENICE:
Well, I were jealous when my foster-brother, Honey, married Clorina. I sent a warning I could tear the ears off her head. But you see I didn't. Clorina's got ears just like anybody else. And now I love her.

FRANKIE [*stopping her walking suddenly*]:
J.A.—Janice and Jarvis. Isn't that the strangest thing?

BERENICE:
What?

FRANKIE:
J.A.—Both their names begin with "J.A."

BERENICE:
And? What about it?

FRANKIE [*walking around the kitchen table*]:
If only my name was Jane. Jane or Jasmine.

BERENICE:
I don't follow your frame of mind.

FRANKIE:
Jarvis and Janice and Jasmine. See?

BERENICE:
No. I don't see.

FRANKIE:

I wonder if it's against the law to change your name. Or add to it.

BERENICE:

Naturally. It's against the law.

FRANKIE [*impetuously*]:

Well, I don't care. F. Jasmine Addams.

JOHN HENRY [*approaching with the doll*]:

You serious when you give me this? [*He pulls up the doll's dress and pats her.*] I will name her Belle.

FRANKIE:

I don't know what went on in Jarvis' mind when he brought me that doll. Imagine bringing me a doll! I had counted on Jarvis bringing me something from Alaska.

BERENICE:

Your face when you unwrapped that package was a study.

FRANKIE:

John Henry, quit pickin' at the doll's eyes. It makes me so nervous. You hear me! [*He sits the doll up.*] In fact, take the doll somewhere out of my sight.

JOHN HENRY:

Her name is Lily Belle.

[*John Henry goes out and props the doll up on the back steps. There is the sound of an unseen Negro singing from the neighboring yard.*]

27

FRANKIE [*going to the mirror*]:
The big mistake I made was to get this close crew cut.
For the wedding, I ought to have long brunette hair.
Don't you think so?

BERENICE:
I don't see how come brunette hair is necessary. But I
warned you about getting your head shaved off like that
before you did it. But nothing would do but you shave it
like that.

FRANKIE [*stepping back from the mirror and slumping
her shoulders*]:
Oh, I am so worried about being so tall. I'm twelve and
five-sixth years old and already five feet five and three-
fourths inches tall. If I keep on growing like this until I'm
twenty-one, I figure I will be nearly ten feet tall.

JOHN HENRY [*re-entering the kitchen*]:
Lily Belle is taking a nap on the back steps. Don't talk so
loud, Frankie.

FRANKIE [*after a pause*]:
I doubt if they ever get married or go to a wedding. Those
freaks.

BERENICE:
Freaks. What freaks you talking about?

FRANKIE:
At the fair. The ones we saw there last October.

JOHN HENRY:
Oh, the freaks at the fair! [*He holds out an imaginary
skirt and begins to skip around the room with one finger*

28

*resting on the top of his head.*] Oh, she was the cutest little girl I ever saw. I never saw anything so cute in my whole life. Did you, Frankie?

FRANKIE:
No. I don't think she was cute.

BERENICE:
Who is that he's talking about?

FRANKIE:
That little old pin-head at the fair. A head no bigger than an orange. With the hair shaved off and a big pink bow at the top. Bow was bigger than the head.

JOHN HENRY:
Shoo! She was too cute.

BERENICE:
That little old squeezed-looking midget in them little trick evening clothes. And that giant with the hang-jaw face and them huge loose hands. And that morphidite! Half man—half woman. With that tiger skin on one side and that spangled skirt on the other.

JOHN HENRY:
But that little-headed girl was cute.

FRANKIE:
And that wild colored man they said came from a savage island and ate those real live rats. Do you think they make a very big salary?

BERENICE:
How would I know? In fact, all them freak folks down at the fair every October just gives me the creeps.

FRANKIE [*after a pause, and slowly*]:
Do I give you the creeps?

BERENICE:
You?

FRANKIE:
Do you think I will grow into a freak?

BERENICE:
You? Why certainly not, I trust Jesus!

FRANKIE [*going over to the mirror, and looking at herself*]:
Well, do you think I will be pretty?

BERENICE:
Maybe. If you file down them horns a inch or two.

FRANKIE [*turning to face Berenice, and shuffling one bare foot on the floor*]:
Seriously.

BERENICE:
Seriously, I think when you fill out you will do very well. If you behave.

FRANKIE:
But by Sunday, I want to do something to improve myself before the wedding.

BERENICE:
Get clean for a change. Scrub your elbows and fix yourself nice. You will do very well.

JOHN HENRY:

You will be all right if you file down them horns.

FRANKIE [*raising her right shoulder and turning from the mirror*]:

I don't know what to do. I just wish I would die.

BERENICE:

Well, die then!

JOHN HENRY:

Die.

FRANKIE [*suddenly exasperated*]:

Go home! [*There is a pause.*] You heard me! [*She makes a face at him and threatens him with the fly swatter. They run twice around the table.*] Go home! I'm sick and tired of you, you little midget.

[*John Henry goes out, taking the doll with him.*]

BERENICE:

Now what makes you act like that? You are too mean to live.

FRANKIE:

I know it. [*She takes a carving knife from the table drawer.*] Something about John Henry just gets on my nerves these days. [*She puts her left ankle over her right knee and begins to pick with the knife at a splinter in her foot.*] I've got a splinter in my foot.

BERENICE:

That knife ain't the proper thing for a splinter.

FRANKIE:

It seems to me that before this summer I used always to
have such a good time. Remember this spring when Evelyn Owen and me used to dress up in costumes and go
down town and shop at the five-and-dime? And how
every Friday night we'd spend the night with each other
either at her house or here? And then Evelyn Owen had
to go and move away to Florida. And now she won't even
write to me.

BERENICE:

Honey, you are not crying, is you? Don't that hurt you
none?

FRANKIE:

It would hurt anybody else except me. And how the
wisteria in town was so blue and pretty in April but somehow it was so pretty it made me sad. And how Evelyn
and me put on that show the Glee Club did at the High
School Auditorium? [*She raises her head and beats time
with the knife and her fist on the table, singing loudly
with sudden energy.*] Sons of toil and danger! Will you
serve a stranger! And bow down to Burgundy! [*Berenice
joins in on "Burgundy." Frankie pauses, then begins to
pick her foot again, humming the tune sadly.*]

BERENICE:

That was a nice show you children copied in the arbor.
You will meet another girl friend you like as well as Evelyn
Owen. Or maybe Mr. Owen will move back into town.
[*There is a pause.*] Frankie, what you need is a needle.

FRANKIE:

I don't care anything about my old feet. [*She stomps her
foot on the floor and lays down the knife on the table.*]

32

It was just so queer the way it happened this afternoon. The minute I laid eyes on the pair of them I had this funny feeling. [*She goes over and picks up a saucer of milk near the cat-hole in back of the door and pours the milk in the sink.*] How old were you, Berenice, when you married your first husband?

BERENICE:
I were thirteen years old.

FRANKIE:
What made you get married so young for?

BERENICE:
Because I wanted to.

FRANKIE:
You never loved any of your four husbands but Ludie.

BERENICE:
Ludie Maxwell Freeman was my only true husband. The other ones were just scraps.

FRANKIE:
Did you marry with a veil every time?

BERENICE:
Three times with a veil.

FRANKIE [*pouring milk into the saucer and returning the saucer to the cat-hole*]:
If only I just knew where he is gone. Ps, ps, ps . . . Charles, Charles.

33

BERENICE:

Quit worrying yourself about that old alley cat. He's gone off to hunt a friend.

FRANKIE:

To hunt a friend?

BERENICE:

Why certainly. He roamed off to find himself a lady friend.

FRANKIE:

Well, why don't he bring his friend home with him? He ought to know I would be only too glad to have a whole family of cats.

BERENICE:

You done seen the last of that old alley cat.

FRANKIE [*crossing the room*]:

I ought to notify the police force. They will find Charles.

BERENICE:

I wouldn't do that.

FRANKIE [*at the telephone*]:

I want the police force, please . . . Police force? . . . I am notifying you about my cat . . . Cat! He's lost. He is almost pure Persian.

BERENICE:

As Persian as I is.

FRANKIE:

But with short hair. A lovely color of gray with a little white spot on his throat. He answers to the name of

Charles, but if he don't answer to that, he might come if you call "Charlina." . . . My name is Miss F. Jasmine Addams and the address is 124 Grove Street.

BERENICE [*giggling as Frankie re-enters*]:
Gal, they going to send around here and tie you up and drag you off to Milledgeville. Just picture them fat blue police chasing tomcats around alleys and hollering, "Oh Charles! Oh come here, Charlina!" Merciful Heavens.

FRANKIE:
Aw, shut up!

[*Outside a voice is heard calling in a drawn-out chant, the words almost indistinguishable: "Lot of okra, peas, fresh butter beans . . ."*]

BERENICE:
The trouble with you is that you don't have no sense of humor no more.

FRANKIE [*disconsolately*]:
Maybe I'd be better off in jail.

[*The chanting voice continues and an ancient Negro woman, dressed in a clean print dress with several petticoats, the ruffle of one of which shows, crosses the yard. She stops and leans on a gnarled stick.*]

FRANKIE:
Here comes the old vegetable lady.

BERENICE:
Sis Laura is getting mighty feeble to peddle this hot weather.

FRANKIE:

She is about ninety. Other old folks lose their faculties, but she found some faculty. She reads futures, too.

BERENICE:

Hi, Sis Laura. How is your folks getting on?

SIS LAURA:

We ain't much, and I feels my age these days. Want any peas today? [*She shuffles across the yard.*]

BERENICE:

I'm sorry, I still have some left over from yesterday. Good-bye, Sis Laura.

SIS LAURA:

Good-bye. [*She goes off behind the house to the right, continuing her chant.*]

[*When the old woman is gone Frankie begins walking around the kitchen.*]

FRANKIE:

I expect Janice and Jarvis are almost to Winter Hill by now.

BERENICE:

Sit down. You make me nervous.

FRANKIE:

Jarvis talked about Granny. He remembers her very good. But when I try to remember Granny, it is like her face is changing—like a face seen under water. Jarvis remembers Mother too, and I don't remember her at all.

BERENICE:

Naturally! Your mother died the day that you were born.

FRANKIE [*standing with one foot on the seat of the chair, leaning over the chair back and laughing*]:
Did you hear what Jarvis said?

BERENICE:

What?

FRANKIE [*after laughing more*]:
They were talking about whether to vote for C. P. Mac-Donald. And Jarvis said, "Why I wouldn't vote for that scoundrel if he was running to be dogcatcher." I never heard anything so witty in my life. [*There is a silence during which Berenice watches Frankie, but does not smile.*] And you know what Janice remarked. When Jarvis mentioned about how much I've grown, she said she didn't think I looked so terribly big. She said she got the major portion of her growth before she was thirteen. She said I was the right height and had acting talent and ought to go to Hollywood. She did, Berenice.

BERENICE:

O.K. All right! She did!

FRANKIE:

She said she thought I was a lovely size and would probably not grow any taller. She said all fashion models and movie stars . . .

BERENICE:

She did not. I heard her from the window. She only remarked that you probably had already got your growth. But she didn't go on and on like that or mention Hollywood.

FRANKIE:
She said to me . . .

BERENICE:
She said to you! This is a serious fault with you, Frankie.
Somebody just makes a loose remark and then you cozen
it in your mind until nobody would recognize it. Your
Aunt Pet happened to mention to Clorina that you had
sweet manners and Clorina passed it on to you. For what
it was worth. Then next thing I know you are going all
around and bragging how Mrs. West thought you had the
finest manners in town and ought to go to Hollywood,
and I don't know what-all you didn't say. And that is a
serious fault.

FRANKIE:
Aw, quit preaching at me.

BERENICE:
I ain't preaching. It's the solemn truth and you know it.

FRANKIE:
I admit it a little. [*She sits down at the table and puts her
forehead on the palms of her hands. There is a pause, and
then she speaks softly.*] What I need to know is this. Do
you think I made a good impression?

BERENICE:
Impression?

FRANKIE:
Yes.

BERENICE:
Well, how would I know?

38

FRANKIE:
I mean, how did I act? What did I do?

BERENICE:
Why, you didn't do anything to speak of.

FRANKIE:
Nothing?

BERENICE:
No. You just watched the pair of them like they was ghosts. Then, when they talked about the wedding, them ears of yours stiffened out the size of cabbage leaves . . .

FRANKIE [*raising her hand to her ear*]:
They didn't!

BERENICE:
They did.

FRANKIE:
Some day you going to look down and find that big fat tongue of yours pulled out by the roots and laying there before you on the table.

BERENICE:
Quit talking so rude.

FRANKIE [*after a pause*]:
I'm so scared I didn't make a good impression.

BERENICE:
What of it? I got a date with T. T. and he's supposed to pick me up here. I wish him and Honey would come on. You make me nervous.

39

[*Frankie sits miserably, her shoulders hunched. Then with a sudden gesture she bangs her forehead on the table. Her fists are clenched and she is sobbing.*]

BERENICE:

Come on. Don't act like that.

FRANKIE [*her voice muffled*]:

They were so pretty. They must have such a good time. And they went away and left me.

BERENICE:

Sit up. Behave yourself.

FRANKIE:

They came and went away, and left me with this feeling.

BERENICE:

Hosee! I bet I know something. [*She begins tapping with her heel: one, two, three—bang! After a pause, in which the rhythm is established, she begins singing.*] Frankie's got a crush! Frankie's got a crush! Frankie's got a crush on the *wedding!*

FRANKIE:

Quit!

BERENICE:

Frankie's got a crush! Frankie's got a crush!

FRANKIE:

You better quit! [*She rises suddenly and snatches up the carving knife.*]

BERENICE:

You lay down that knife.

**40**

FRANKIE:

Make me. [*She bends the blade slowly.*]

BERENICE:

Lay it down, *Devil*. [*There is a silence.*] Just throw it! You just!

[*After a pause Frankie aims the knife carefully at the closed door leading to the bedroom and throws it. The knife does not stick in the wall.*]

FRANKIE:

I used to be the best knife thrower in this town.

BERENICE:

Frances Addams, you goin' to try that stunt once too often.

FRANKIE:

I warned you to quit pickin' with me.

BERENICE:

You are not fit to live in a house.

FRANKIE:

I won't be living in this one much longer; I'm going to run away from home.

BERENICE:

And a good riddance to a big old bag of rubbage.

FRANKIE:

You wait and see. I'm leaving town.

BERENICE:

And where do you think you are going?

FRANKIE [*gazing around the walls*]:
I don't know.

BERENICE:
You're going crazy. That's where you going.

FRANKIE:
No. [*solemnly*] This coming Sunday after the wedding, I'm leaving town. And I swear to Jesus by my two eyes I'm never coming back here any more.

BERENICE [*going to Frankie and pushing her damp bangs back from her forehead*]:
Sugar? You serious?

FRANKIE [*exasperated*]:
Of course! Do you think I would stand here and say that swear and tell a story? Sometimes, Berenice, I think it takes you longer to realize a fact than it does anybody who ever lived.

BERENICE:
But you say you don't know where you going. You going, but you don't know where. That don't make no sense to me.

FRANKIE [*after a long pause in which she again gazes around the walls of the room*]:
I feel just exactly like somebody has peeled all the skin off me. I wish I had some good cold peach ice cream. [*Berenice takes her by the shoulders.*]

[*During the last speech, T. T. Williams and Honey Camden Brown have been approaching through the back yard. T. T. is a large and pompous-looking Negro*]

42

*man of about fifty. He is dressed like a church deacon,
in a black suit with a red emblem in the lapel. His manner is timid and over-polite. Honey is a slender, limber
Negro boy of about twenty. He is quite light in color
and he wears loud-colored, snappy clothes. He is
brusque and there is about him an odd mixture of hos-
tility and playfulness. He is very high-strung and vola-
tile. They are trailed by John Henry. John Henry is
dressed for afternoon in a clean white linen suit, white
shoes and socks. Honey carries a horn. They cross the
back yard and knock at the back door. Honey holds his
hand to his head.]*

FRANKIE:

But every word I told you was the solemn truth. I'm
leaving here after the wedding.

BERENICE [*taking her hands from Frankie's shoulders
and answering the door*]:
Hello, Honey and T. T. I didn't hear you coming.

T. T.:

You and Frankie too busy discussing something. Well,
your foster-brother, Honey, got into a ruckus standing
on the sidewalk in front of the Blue Moon Café. Police
cracked him on the haid.

BERENICE [*turning on the kitchen light*]:
What! [*She examines Honey's head.*] Why, it's a welt the
size of a small egg.

HONEY:

Times like this I feel like I got to bust loose or die.

BERENICE:
What were you doing?

43

HONEY:

Nothing. I was just passing along the street minding my own business when this drunk soldier came out of the Blue Moon Café and ran into me. I looked at him and he gave me a push. I pushed him back and he raised a ruckus. This white M.P. came up and slammed me with his stick.

T. T.:

It was one of those accidents can happen to any colored person.

JOHN HENRY [*reaching for the horn*]:
Toot some on your horn, Honey.

FRANKIE:

Please blow.

HONEY [*to John Henry, who has taken the horn*]:
Now, don't bother my horn, Butch.

JOHN HENRY:

I want to toot it some.

[*John Henry takes the horn, tries to blow it, but only succeeds in slobbering in it. He holds the horn away from his mouth and sings: "Too-ty-toot, too-ty-toot." Honey snatches the horn away from him and puts it on the sewing table.*]

HONEY:

I told you not to touch my horn. You got it full of slobber inside and out. It's ruined! [*He loses his temper, grabs John Henry by the shoulders and shakes him hard.*]

BERENICE [*slapping Honey*]:
Satan! Don't you dare touch that little boy! I'm going to stomp out your brains!

HONEY:

You ain't mad because John Henry is a little boy. It's because he's a white boy. John Henry knows he needs a good shake. Don't you, Butch?

BERENICE:

Ornery—no good!

[*Honey lifts John Henry and swings him, then reaches in his pocket and brings out some coins.*]

HONEY:

John Henry, which would you rather have—the nigger money or the white money?

JOHN HENRY:

I rather have the dime. [*He takes it.*] Much obliged. [*He goes out and crosses the yard to his house.*]

BERENICE:

You troubled and beat down and try to take it out on a little boy. You and Frankie just alike. The club girls don't elect her and she turns on John Henry too. When folks are lonesome and left out, they turn so mean. T. T. do you wish a small little quickie before we start?

T. T. [*looking at Frankie and pointing toward her*]:
Frankie ain't no tattle-tale. Is you? [*Berenice pours a drink for T. T.*]

FRANKIE [*disdaining his question*]:
That sure is a cute suit you got on, Honey. Today I heard somebody speak of you as Lightfoot Brown. I think that's such a grand nickname. It's on account of your travelling —to Harlem, and all the different places where you have

45

run away, and your dancing. Lightfoot! I wish somebody would call me Lightfoot Addams.

BERENICE:

It would suit me better if Honey Camden had brick feets. As it is, he keeps me so anxious-worried. C'mon, Honey and T. T. Let's go! [*Honey and T. T. go out.*]

FRANKIE:

I'll go out into the yard.

[*Frankie, feeling excluded, goes out into the yard. Throughout the act the light in the yard has been darkening steadily. Now the light in the kitchen is throwing a yellow rectangle in the yard.*]

BERENICE:

Now Frankie, you forget all that foolishness we were discussing. And if Mr. Addams don't come home by good dark, you go over to the Wests'. Go play with John Henry.

HONEY AND T. T. [*from outside*]:

So long!

FRANKIE:

So long, you all. Since when have I been scared of the dark? I'll invite John Henry to spend the night with me.

BERENICE:

I thought you were sick and tired of him.

FRANKIE:

I am.

BERENICE [*kissing Frankie*]:

Good night, Sugar!

FRANKIE:

Seems like everybody goes off and leaves me. [*She walks towards the Wests' yard, calling, with cupped hands.*] John Henry. John Henry.

JOHN HENRY'S VOICE:

What do you want, Frankie?

FRANKIE:

Come over and spend the night with me.

JOHN HENRY'S VOICE:

I can't.

FRANKIE:

Why?

JOHN HENRY:

Just because.

FRANKIE:

Because why? [*John Henry does not answer.*] I thought maybe me and you could put up my Indian tepee and sleep out here in the yard. And have a good time. [*There is still no answer.*] Sure enough. Why don't you stay and spend the night?

JOHN HENRY [*quite loudly*]:

Because, Frankie. I don't want to.

FRANKIE [*angrily*]:

Fool Jackass! Suit yourself! I only asked you because you looked so ugly and so lonesome.

JOHN HENRY [*skipping toward the arbor*]:

Why, I'm not a bit lonesome.

47

FRANKIE [*looking at the house*]:
I wonder when that Papa of mine is coming home. He always comes home by dark. I don't want to go into that empty, ugly house all by myself.

JOHN HENRY:
Me neither.

FRANKIE [*standing with outstretched arms, and looking around her*]:
I think something is wrong. It is too quiet. I have a peculiar warning in my bones. I bet you a hundred dollars it's going to storm.

JOHN HENRY:
I don't want to spend the night with you.

FRANKIE:
A terrible, terrible dog-day storm. Or maybe even a cyclone.

JOHN HENRY:
Huh.

FRANKIE:
I bet Jarvis and Janice are now at Winter Hill. I see them just plain as I see you. Plainer. Something is wrong. It is too quiet.

[*A clear horn begins to play a blues tune in the distance.*]

JOHN HENRY:
Frankie?

FRANKIE:
Hush! It sounds like Honey.

[*The horn music becomes jazzy and spangling, then the first blues tune is repeated. Suddenly, while still unfinished, the music stops. Frankie waits tensely.*]

FRANKIE:
He has stopped to bang the spit out of his horn. In a second he will finish. [*after a wait*] Please, Honey, go on finish!

JOHN HENRY [*softly*]:
He done quit now.

FRANKIE [*moving restlessly*]:
I told Berenice that I was leavin' town for good and she did not believe me. Sometimes I honestly think she is the biggest fool that ever drew breath. You try to impress something on a big fool like that, and it's just like talking to a block of cement. I kept on telling and telling and telling her. I told her I had to leave this town for good because it is inevitable. Inevitable.

[*Mr. Addams enters the kitchen from the house, calling: "Frankie, Frankie."*]

MR. ADDAMS [*calling from the kitchen door*]:
Frankie, Frankie.

FRANKIE:
Yes, Papa.

MR. ADDAMS [*opening the back door*]:
You had supper?

FRANKIE:
I'm not hungry.

MR. ADDAMS:
Was a little later than I intended, fixing a timepiece for a railroad man. [*He goes back through the kitchen and into the hall, calling: "Don't leave the yard!"*]

JOHN HENRY:
You want me to get the weekend bag?

FRANKIE:
Don't bother me, John Henry. I'm thinking.

JOHN HENRY:
What you thinking about?

FRANKIE:
About the wedding. About my brother and the bride. Everything's been so sudden today. I never believed before about the fact that the earth turns at the rate of about a thousand miles a day. I didn't understand why it was that if you jumped up in the air you wouldn't land in Selma or Fairview or somewhere else instead of the same back yard. But now it seems to me I feel the world going around very fast. [*Frankie begins turning around in circles with arms outstretched. John Henry copies her. They both turn.*] I feel it turning and it makes me dizzy.

JOHN HENRY:
I'll stay and spend the night with you.

FRANKIE [*suddenly stopping her turning*]:
No. I just now thought of something.

50

JOHN HENRY:
You just a little while ago was begging me.

FRANKIE:
I know where I'm going.

[*There are sounds of children playing in the distance.*]

JOHN HENRY:
Let's go play with the children, Frankie.

FRANKIE:
I tell you I know where I'm going. It's like I've known it all my life. Tomorrow I will tell everybody.

JOHN HENRY:
Where?

FRANKIE [*dreamily*]:
After the wedding I'm going with them to Winter Hill. I'm going off with them after the wedding.

JOHN HENRY:
You serious?

FRANKIE:
Shush, just now I realized something. The trouble with me is that for a long time I have been just an "I" person. All other people can say "we." When Berenice says "we" she means her lodge and church and colored people. Soldiers can say "we" and mean the army. All people belong to a "we" except me.

JOHN HENRY:
What are we going to do?

51

FRANKIE:

Not to belong to a "we" makes you too lonesome. Until this afternoon I didn't have a "we," but now after seeing Janice and Jarvis I suddenly realize something.

JOHN HENRY:

What?

FRANKIE:

I know that the bride and my brother are the "we" of me. So I'm going with them, and joining with the wedding. This coming Sunday when my brother and the bride leave this town, I'm going with the two of them to Winter Hill. And after that to whatever place that they will ever go. [*There is a pause.*] I love the two of them so much and we belong to be together. I love the two of them so much because they are the *we* of me.

[*The curtain falls.*]

*The scene is the same: the kitchen of the Addams home.
Berenice is cooking. John Henry sits on the stool, blowing
soap bubbles with a spool. It is the afternoon of the next
day.*

[*The front door slams and Frankie enters from the hall.*]

BERENICE:

I been phoning all over town trying to locate you. Where
on earth have you been?

FRANKIE:

Everywhere. All over town.

BERENICE:

I been so worried I got a good mind to be seriously mad
with you. Your Papa came home to dinner today. He was
mad when you didn't show up. He's taking a nap now
in his room.

FRANKIE:

I walked up and down Main Street and stopped in
almost every store. Bought my wedding dress and silver
shoes. Went around by the mills. Went all over the com-
plete town and talked to nearly everybody in it.

BERENICE:
What for, pray tell me?

FRANKIE:

I was telling everybody about the wedding and my plans.
[*She takes off her dress and remains barefooted in her
slip.*]

BERENICE:

You mean just people on the street? [*She is creaming butter and sugar for cookies.*]

FRANKIE:

Everybody. Storekeepers. The monkey and monkey-man. A soldier. Everybody. And you know the soldier wanted to join with me and asked me for a date this evening. I wonder what you do on dates.

BERENICE:

Frankie, I honestly believe you have turned crazy on us. Walking all over town and telling total strangers this big tale. You know in your soul this mania of yours is pure foolishness.

FRANKIE:

Please call me F. Jasmine. I don't wish to have to remind you any more. Everything good of mine has got to be washed and ironed so I can pack them in the suitcase. [*She brings in a suitcase and opens it.*] Everybody in town believes that I'm going. All except Papa. He's stubborn as an old mule. No use arguing with people like that.

BERENICE:

Me and Mr. Addams has some sense.

FRANKIE:

Papa was bent over working on a watch when I went by the store. I asked him could I buy the wedding clothes and he said charge them at MacDougals. But he wouldn't listen to any of my plans. Just sat there with his nose to the grindstone and answered with—kind of grunts. He never listens to what I say. [*There is a pause.*] Sometimes I wonder if Papa loves me or not.

BERENICE:

Course he loves you. He is just a busy widowman—set in his ways.

FRANKIE:

Now I wonder if I can find some tissue paper to line this suitcase.

BERENICE:

Truly, Frankie, what makes you think they want you taggin' along with them? Two is company and three is a crowd. And that's the main thing about a wedding. Two is company and three is a crowd.

FRANKIE:

You wait and see.

BERENICE:

Remember back to the time of the flood. Remember Noah and the Ark.

FRANKIE:

And what has that got to do with it?

BERENICE:

Remember the way he admitted them creatures.

FRANKIE:

Oh, shut up your big old mouth!

BERENICE:

Two by two. He admitted them creatures two by two.

FRANKIE [after a pause]:

That's all right. But you wait and see. They will take me.

55

BERENICE:
And if they don't?

FRANKIE [*turning suddenly from washing her hands at the sink*]:
If they don't, I will kill myself.

BERENICE:
Kill yourself, how?

FRANKIE:
I will shoot myself in the side of the head with the pistol that Papa keeps under his handkerchiefs with Mother's picture in the bureau drawer.

BERENICE:
You heard what Mr. Addams said about playing with that pistol. I'll just put this cookie dough in the icebox. Set the table and your dinner is ready. Set John Henry a plate and one for me. [*Berenice puts the dough in the icebox. Frankie hurriedly sets the table. Berenice takes dishes from the stove and ties a napkin around John Henry's neck.*] I have heard of many a peculiar thing. I have knew men to fall in love with girls so ugly that you wonder if their eyes is straight.

JOHN HENRY:
Who?

BERENICE:
I have knew women to love veritable satans and thank Jesus when they put their split hooves over the threshold. I have knew boys to take it into their heads to fall in love with other boys. You know Lily Mae Jenkins?

56

FRANKIE:
I'm not sure. I know a lot of people.

BERENICE:
Well, you either know him or you don't know him. He prisses around in a girl's blouse with one arm akimbo. Now this Lily Mae Jenkins fell in love with a man name Juney Jones. A man, mind you. And Lily Mae turned into a girl. He changed his nature and his sex and turned into a girl.

FRANKIE:
What?

BERENICE:
He did. To all intents and purposes. [*Berenice is sitting in the center chair at the table. She says grace.*] Lord, make us thankful for what we are about to receive to nourish our bodies. Amen.

FRANKIE:
It's funny I can't think who you are talking about. I used to think I knew so many people.

BERENICE:
Well, you don't need to know Lily Mae Jenkins. You can live without knowing him.

FRANKIE:
Anyway, I don't believe you.

BERENICE:
I ain't arguing with you. What was we speaking about?

FRANKIE:
About peculiar things.

57

BERENICE:

Oh, yes. As I was just now telling you I have seen many a peculiar thing in my day. But one thing I never knew and never heard tell about. No, siree. I never in all my days heard of anybody falling in love with a wedding. [*There is a pause.*] And thinking it all over I have come to a conclusion.

JOHN HENRY:

How? How did that boy change into a girl? Did he kiss his elbow? [*He tries to kiss his elbow.*]

BERENICE:

It was just one of them things, Candy Lamb. Yep, I have come to the conclusion that what you ought to be thinking about is a beau. A nice little white boy beau.

FRANKIE:

I don't want any beau. What would I do with one? Do you mean something like a soldier who would maybe take me to the Idle Hour?

BERENICE:

Who's talking about soldiers? I'm talking about a nice little white boy beau your own age. How 'bout that little old Barney next door?

FRANKIE:

Barney MacKean! That nasty Barney!

BERENICE:

Certainly! You could make out with him until somebody better comes along. He would do.

FRANKIE:
You are the biggest crazy in this town.

BERENICE:
The crazy calls the sane the crazy.

[*Barney MacKean, a boy of twelve, shirtless and wearing shorts, and Helen Fletcher, a girl of twelve or fourteen, cross the yard from the left, go through the arbor and out on the right. Frankie and John Henry watch them from the window.*]

FRANKIE:
Yonder's Barney now with Helen Fletcher. They are going to the alley behind the Wests' garage. They do something bad back there. I don't know what it is.

BERENICE:
If you don't know what it is, how come you know it is bad?

FRANKIE:
I just know it. I think maybe they look at each other and peepee or something. They don't let anybody watch them.

JOHN HENRY:
I watched them once.

FRANKIE:
What do they do?

JOHN HENRY:
I saw. They don't peepee.

FRANKIE:
Then what do they do?

JOHN HENRY:

I don't know what it was. But I watched them. How many of them did you catch, Berenice? Them beaus?

BERENICE:

How many? Candy Lamb, how many hairs is in this plait? You're talking to Miss Berenice Sadie Brown.

FRANKIE:

I think you ought to quit worrying about beaus and be content with T. T. I bet you are forty years old.

BERENICE:

Wise-mouth. How do you know so much? I got as much right as anybody else to continue to have a good time as long as I can. And as far as that goes, I'm not so old as some peoples would try and make out. I ain't changed life yet.

JOHN HENRY:

Did they all treat you to the picture show, them beaus?

BERENICE:

To the show, or one thing or another. Wipe off your mouth.

[*There is the sound of piano tuning.*]

JOHN HENRY:

The piano tuning man.

BERENICE:

Ye Gods, I seriously believe this will be the last straw.

JOHN HENRY:

Me too.

FRANKIE:

It makes me sad. And jittery too. [*She walks around the room.*] They tell me that when they want to punish the crazy people in Milledgeville, they tie them up and make them listen to piano tuning. [*She puts the empty coal scuttle on her head and walks around the table.*]

BERENICE:

We could turn on the radio and drown him out.

FRANKIE:

I don't want the radio on. [*She goes into the interior room and takes off her dress, speaking from inside.*] But I advise you to keep the radio on after I leave. Some day you will very likely hear us speak over the radio.

BERENICE:

Speak about what, pray tell me?

FRANKIE:

I don't know exactly what about. But probably some eye witness account about something. We will be asked to speak.

BERENICE:

I don't follow you. What are we going to eye witness? And who will ask us to speak?

JOHN HENRY [*excitedly*]:

What, Frankie? Who is speaking on the radio?

FRANKIE:

When I said *we*, you thought I meant you and me and John Henry West. To speak over the world radio. I have never heard of anything so funny since I was born.

JOHN HENRY [*climbing up to kneel on the seat of the chair*]:
Who? What?

FRANKIE:
Ha! Ha! Ho! Ho! Ho! Ho!

[*Frankie goes around punching things with her fist, and shadow boxing. Berenice raises her right hand for peace. Then suddenly they all stop. Frankie goes to the window, and John Henry hurries there also and stands on tiptoe with his hands on the sill. Berenice turns her head to see what has happened. The piano is still. Three young girls in clean dresses are passing before the arbor. Frankie watches them silently at the window.*]

JOHN HENRY [*softly*]:
The club of girls.

FRANKIE:
What do you son-of-a-bitches mean crossing my yard? How many times must I tell you not to set foot on my Papa's property?

BERENICE:
Just ignore them and make like you don't see them pass.

FRANKIE:
Don't mention those crooks to me.

[*T. T. and Honey approach by way of the back yard. Honey is whistling a blues tune.*]

BERENICE:
Why don't you show me the new dress? I'm anxious to see what you selected. [*Frankie goes into the interior*

62

*room. T. T. knocks on the door. He and Honey enter.*]
Why T. T. what you doing around here this time of day?

T. T.:
Good afternoon, Miss Berenice. I'm here on a sad mission.

BERENICE [*startled*]:
What's wrong?

T. T.:
It's about Sis Laura Thompson. She suddenly had a stroke
and died.

BERENICE:
What! Why she was by here just yesterday. We just
ate her peas. They in my stomach right now, and her lyin'
dead on the cooling board this minute. The Lord works
in strange ways.

T. T.:
Passed away at dawn this morning.

FRANKIE [*putting her head in the doorway*]:
Who is it that's dead?

BERENICE:
Sis Laura, Sugar. That old vegetable lady.

FRANKIE [*unseen, from the interior room*]:
Just to think—she passed by yesterday.

T. T.:
Miss Berenice, I'm going around to take up a donation for
the funeral. The policy people say Sis Laura's claim has
lapsed.

63

BERENICE:

Well, here's fifty cents. The poor old soul.

T. T.:

She was brisk as a chipmunk to the last. The Lord had appointed the time for her. I hope I go that way.

FRANKIE [*from the interior room*]:

I've got something to show you all. Shut your eyes and don't open them until I tell you. [*She enters the room dressed in an orange satin evening dress with silver shoes and stockings.*] These are the wedding clothes. [*Berenice, T. T. and John Henry stare.*]

JOHN HENRY:

Oh, how pretty!

FRANKIE:

Now tell me your honest opinion. [*There is a pause.*] What's the matter? Don't you like it, Berenice?

BERENICE:

No. It don't do.

FRANKIE:

What do you mean? It don't do.

BERENICE:

Exactly that. It just don't do. [*She shakes her head while Frankie looks at the dress.*]

FRANKIE:

But I don't see what you mean. What is wrong?

BERENICE:

Well, if you don't see it I can't explain it to you. Look there at your head, to begin with. [*Frankie goes to the*

64

*mirror.*] You had all your hair shaved off like a convict and now you tie this ribbon around this head without any hair. Just looks peculiar.

FRANKIE:
But I'm going to wash and try to stretch my hair tonight.

BERENICE:
Stretch your hair! How you going to stretch your hair? And look at them elbows. Here you got on a grown woman's evening dress. And that brown crust on your elbows. The two things just don't mix. [*Frankie, embarrassed, covers her elbows with her hands. Berenice is still shaking her head.*] Take it back down to the store.

T. T.:
The dress is too growny looking.

FRANKIE:
But I can't take it back. It's bargain basement.

BERENICE:
Very well then. Come here. Let me see what I can do.

FRANKIE [*going to Berenice, who works with the dress*]:
I think you're just not accustomed to seeing anybody dressed up.

BERENICE:
I'm not accustomed to seein' a human Christmas tree in August.

JOHN HENRY:
Frankie's dress looks like a Christmas tree.

65

FRANKIE:

Two-faced Judas! You just now said it was pretty. Old double-faced Judas! [*The sounds of piano tuning are heard again.*] Oh, that piano tuner!

BERENICE:

Step back a little now.

FRANKIE [*looking in the mirror*]:

Don't you honestly think it's pretty? Give me your candy opinion.

BERENICE:

I never knew anybody so unreasonable! You ask me my candy opinion, I give you my candy opinion. You ask me again, and I give it to you again. But what you want is not my honest opinion, but my good opinion of something I know is wrong.

FRANKIE:

I only want to look pretty.

BERENICE:

Pretty is as pretty does. Ain't that right, T. T.? You will look well enough for anybody's wedding. Excepting your own.

[*Mr. Addams enters through the hall door.*]

MR. ADDAMS:

Hello, everybody. [*to Frankie*] I don't want you roaming around the streets all morning and not coming home at dinner time. Looks like I'll have to tie you up in the back yard.

FRANKIE:

I had business to tend to. Papa, look!

MR. ADDAMS:

What is it, Miss Picklepriss?

FRANKIE:

Sometimes I think you have turned stone blind. You never even noticed my new dress.

MR. ADDAMS:

I thought it was a show costume.

FRANKIE:

Show costume! Papa, why is it you don't ever notice what I have on or pay any serious mind to me? You just walk around like a mule with blinders on, not seeing or caring.

MR. ADDAMS:

Never mind that now. [to T. T. and Honey] I need some help down at my store. My porter failed me again. I wonder if you or Honey could help me next week.

T. T.:

I will if I can, sir, Mr. Addams. What days would be convenient for you, sir?

MR. ADDAMS:

Say Wednesday afternoon.

T. T.:

Now, Mr. Addams, that's one afternoon I promised to work for Mr. Finny, sir. I can't promise anything, Mr. Addams. But if Mr. Finny change his mind about needing me, I'll work for you, sir.

MR. ADDAMS:
How about you, Honey?

HONEY [*shortly*]:
I ain't got the time.

MR. ADDAMS:
I'll be so glad when the war is over and you biggety, worthless niggers get back to work. And, furthermore, you *sir* me! Hear me?

HONEY [*reluctantly*]:
Yes,—sir.

MR. ADDAMS:
I better go back to the store now and get my nose down to the grindstone. You stay home, Frankie. [*He goes out through the hall door.*]

JOHN HENRY:
Uncle Royal called Honey a nigger. Is Honey a nigger?

BERENICE:
Be quiet now, John Henry. [*to Honey*] Honey, I got a good mind to shake you till you spit. Not saying *sir* to Mr. Addams, and acting so impudent.

HONEY:
T. T. said sir enough for a whole crowd of niggers. But for folks that calls me nigger, I got a real good nigger razor. [*He takes a razor from his pocket. Frankie and John Henry crowd close to look. When John Henry touches the razor Honey says:*] Don't touch it, Butch, it's sharp. Liable to hurt yourself.

BERENICE:

Put up that razor, Satan! I worry myself sick over you. You going to die before your appointed span.

JOHN HENRY:

Why is Honey a nigger?

BERENICE:

Jesus knows.

HONEY:

I'm so tensed up. My nerves been scraped with a razor. Berenice, loan me a dollar.

BERENICE:

I ain't handing you no dollar, worthless, to get high on them reefer cigarettes.

HONEY:

Gimme, Berenice, I'm so tensed up and miserable. The nigger hole. I'm sick of smothering in the nigger hole. I can't stand it no more.

[*Relenting, Berenice gets her pocketbook from the shelf, opens it, and takes out some change.*]

BERENICE:

Here's thirty cents. You can buy two beers.

HONEY:

Well, thankful for tiny, infinitesimal favors. I better be dancing off now.

T. T.:

Same here. I still have to make a good deal of donation visits this afternoon. [*Honey and T. T. go to the door.*]

69

BERENICE:

So long, T. T. I'm counting on you for tomorrow and you too, Honey.

FRANKIE and JOHN HENRY:

So long.

T. T.:

Good-bye, you all. Good-bye. [*He goes out, crossing the yard.*]

BERENICE:

Poor ole Sis Laura. I certainly hope that when my time comes I will have kept up my policy. I dread to think the church would ever have to bury me. When I die.

JOHN HENRY:

Are you going to die, Berenice?

BERENICE:

Why, Candy, everybody has to die.

JOHN HENRY:

Everybody? Are you going to die, Frankie?

FRANKIE:

I doubt it. I honestly don't think I'll ever die.

JOHN HENRY:

What is "die"?

FRANKIE:

It must be terrible to be nothing but black, black, black.

BERENICE:

Yes, baby.

FRANKIE:

How many dead people do you know? I know six dead people in all. I'm not counting my mother. There's William Boyd who was killed in Italy. I knew him by sight and name. An' that man who climbed poles for the telephone company. An' Lou Baker. The porter at Finny's place who was murdered in the alley back of Papa's store. Somebody drew a razor on him and the alley people said that his cut throat shivered like a mouth and spoke ghost words to the sun.

JOHN HENRY:

Ludie Maxwell Freeman is dead.

FRANKIE:

I didn't count Ludie; it wouldn't be fair. Because he died just before I was born. [to Berenice] Do you think very frequently about Ludie?

BERENICE:

You know I do. I think about the five years when me and Ludie was together, and about all the bad times I seen since. Sometimes I almost wish I had never knew Ludie at all. It leaves you too lonesome afterward. When you walk home in the evening on the way from work, it makes a little lonesome quinch come in you. And you take up with too many sorry men to try to get over the feeling.

FRANKIE:

But T. T. is not sorry.

BERENICE:

I wasn't referring to T. T. He is a fine upstanding colored gentleman, who has walked in a state of grace all his life.

FRANKIE:

When are you going to marry with him?

BERENICE:

I ain't going to marry with him.

FRANKIE:

But you were just now saying . . .

BERENICE:

I was saying how sincerely I respect T. T. and sincerely regard T. T. [*There is a pause.*] But he don't make me shiver none.

FRANKIE:

Listen, Berenice, I have something queer to tell you. It's something that happened when I was walking around town today. Now I don't exactly know how to explain what I mean.

BERENICE:
What is it?

FRANKIE [*now and then pulling her bangs or lower lip*]: I was walking along and I passed two stores with a alley in between. The sun was frying hot. And just as I passed this alley, I caught a *glimpse* of something in the corner of my left eye. A dark double shape. And this glimpse brought to my mind—so sudden and clear—my brother and the bride that I just stood there and couldn't hardly bear to look and see what it was. It was like they were there in that alley, although I knew that they are in Winter Hill almost a hundred miles away. [*There is a pause.*] Then I turn slowly and look. And you know what was there? [*There is a pause.*] It was just two colored boys. That was all. But it gave me such a queer feeling.

[*Berenice has been listening attentively. She stares at Frankie, then draws a package of cigarettes from her bosom and lights one.*]

BERENICE:

Listen at me! Can you see through these bones in my forehead? [*She points to her forehead.*] Have you, Frankie Addams, been reading my mind? [*There is a pause.*] That's the most remarkable thing I ever heard of.

FRANKIE:

What I mean is that . . .

BERENICE:

I know what you mean. You mean right here in the corner of your eye. [*She points to her eye.*] You suddenly catch something there. And this cold shiver run all the way down you. And you whirl around. And you stand there facing Jesus knows what. But not Ludie, not who you want. And for a minute you feel like you been dropped down a well.

FRANKIE:

Yes. That is it. [*Frankie reaches for a cigarette and lights it, coughing a bit.*]

BERENICE:

Well, that is mighty remarkable. This is a thing been happening to me all my life. Yet just now is the first time I ever heard it put into words. [*There is a pause.*] Yes, that is the way it is when you are in love. A thing known and not spoken.

FRANKIE [*patting her foot*]:

Yet I always maintained I never believed in love. I didn't admit it and never put any of it in my shows.

73

JOHN HENRY:
I never believed in love.

BERENICE:
Now I will tell you something. And it is to be a warning to you. You hear me, John Henry. You hear me, Frankie.

JOHN HENRY:
Yes. [*He points his forefinger.*] Frankie is smoking.

BERENICE [*squaring her shoulders*]:
Now I am here to tell you I was happy. There was no human woman in all the world more happy than I was in them days. And that includes everybody. You listening to me, John Henry? It includes all queens and millionaires and first ladies of the land. And I mean it includes people of all color. You hear me, Frankie? No human woman in all the world was happier than Berenice Sadie Brown.

FRANKIE:
The five years you were married to Ludie.

BERENICE:
From that autumn morning when I first met him on the road in front of Campbell's Filling Station until the very night he died, November, the year 1933.

FRANKIE:
The very year and the very month I was born.

BERENICE:
The coldest November I ever seen. Every morning there was frost and puddles were crusted with ice. The sunshine was pale yellow like it is in winter time. Sounds carried far away, and I remember a hound dog that used to howl

toward sundown. And everything I seen come to me as a kind of sign.

FRANKIE:

I think it is a kind of sign I was born the same year and the same month he died.

BERENICE:

And it was a Thursday towards six o'clock. About this time of day. Only November. I remember I went to the passage and opened the front door. Dark was coming on; the old hound was howling far away. And I go back in the room and lay down on Ludie's bed. I lay myself down over Ludie with my arms spread out and my face on his face. And I pray that the Lord would contage my strength to him. And I ask the Lord let it be anybody, but not let it be Ludie. And I lay there and pray for a long time. Until night.

JOHN HENRY:

How? [*in a higher, wailing voice*] How, Berenice?

BERENICE:

That night he died. I tell you he died. Ludie! Ludie Freeman! Ludie Maxwell Freeman died! [*She hums.*]

FRANKIE [*after a pause*]:

It seems to me I feel sadder about Ludie than any other dead person. Although I never knew him. I know I ought to cry sometimes about my mother, or anyhow Granny. But it looks like I can't. But Ludie—maybe it was because I was born so soon after Ludie died. But you were starting out to tell some kind of a warning.

BERENICE [*looking puzzled for a moment*]:
Warning? Oh, yes! I was going to tell you how this thing
we was talking about applies to me. [*As Berenice begins to
talk Frankie goes to a shelf above the refrigerator and
brings back a fig bar to the table.*] It was the April of the
following year that I went one Sunday to the church
where the congregation was strange to me. I had my forehead down on the top of the pew in front of me, and my
eyes were open—not peeping around in secret, mind you,
but just open. When suddenly this shiver ran all the way
through me. I had caught sight of something from the
corner of my eye. And I looked slowly to the left. There
on the pew, just six inches from my eyes, was this *thumb*.

FRANKIE:
What thumb?

BERENICE:
Now I have to tell you. There was only one small portion
of Ludie Freeman which was not pretty. Every other part
about him was handsome and pretty as anyone would wish.
All except this right thumb. This one thumb had a mashed,
chewed appearance that was not pretty. You understand?

FRANKIE:
You mean you suddenly saw Ludie's thumb when you
were praying?

BERENICE:
I mean I seen *this* thumb. And as I knelt there just staring
at this thumb, I begun to pray in earnest. I prayed out
loud! Lord, manifest! Lord, manifest!

FRANKIE:
And did He—manifest?

76

BERENICE:

Manifest, my foot! [*spitting*] You know who that thumb belonged to?

FRANKIE:

Who?

BERENICE:

Why, Jamie Beale. That big old no-good Jamie Beale. It was the first time I ever laid eyes on him.

FRANKIE:

Is that why you married him? Because he had a mashed thumb like Ludie's?

BERENICE:

Lord only knows. I don't. I guess I felt drawn to him on account of that thumb. And then one thing led to another. First thing I know I had married him.

FRANKIE:

Well, I think that was silly. To marry him just because of that thumb.

BERENICE:

I'm not trying to dispute with you. I'm just telling you what actually happened. And the very same thing occurred in the case of Henry Johnson.

FRANKIE:

You mean to sit there and tell me Henry Johnson had one of those mashed thumbs too?

BERENICE:

No. It was not the thumb this time. It was the coat. [*Frankie and John Henry look at each other in amaze-*

77

*ment. After a pause Berenice continues.*] Now when Ludie died, them policy people cheated me out of fifty dollars so I pawned everything I could lay hands on, and I sold my coat and Ludie's coat. Because I couldn't let Ludie be put away cheap.

FRANKIE:

Oh! Then you mean Henry Johnson bought Ludie's coat and you married him because of it?

BERENICE:

Not exactly. I was walking down the street one evening when I suddenly seen this shape appear before me. Now the shape of this boy ahead of me was so similar to Ludie through the shoulders and the back of the head that I almost dropped dead there on the sidewalk. I followed and run behind him. It was Henry Johnson. Since he lived in the country and didn't come into town, he had chanced to buy Ludie's coat and from the back view it looked like he was Ludie's ghost or Ludie's twin. But how I married him I don't exactly know, for, to begin with, it was clear that he did not have his share of sense. But you let a boy hang around and you get fond of him. Anyway, that's how I married Henry Johnson.

FRANKIE:

He was the one went crazy on you. Had eatin' dreams and swallowed the corner of the sheet. [*There is a pause.*] But I don't understand the point of what you was telling. I don't see how that about Jamie Beale and Henry Johnson applies to me.

BERENICE:

Why, it applies to everybody and it is a warning.

78

FRANKIE:
But how?

BERENICE:
Why, Frankie, don't you see what I was doing? I loved
Ludie and he was the first man I loved. Therefore I had
to go and copy myself forever afterward. What I did was
to marry off little pieces of Ludie whenever I come across
them. It was just my misfortune they all turned out to be
the wrong pieces. My intention was to repeat me and
Ludie. Now don't you see?

FRANKIE:
I see what you're driving at. But I don't see how it is a
warning applied to me.

BERENICE:
You don't! Then I'll tell you. [*Frankie does not nod or
answer. The piano tuner plays an arpeggio.*] You and that
wedding tomorrow. That is what I am warning about.
I can see right through them two gray eyes of yours like
they was glass. And what I see is the saddest piece of foolishness I ever knew.

JOHN HENRY [*in a low voice*]:
Gray eyes is glass.

[*Frankie tenses her brows and looks steadily at Berenice.*]

BERENICE:
I see what you have in mind. Don't think I don't. You see
something unheard of tomorrow, and you right in the
center. You think you going to march to the preacher

79

right in between your brother and the bride. You think you going to break into that wedding, and then Jesus knows what else.

FRANKIE:
No. I don't see myself walking to the preacher with them.

BERENICE:
I see through them eyes. Don't argue with me.

JOHN HENRY [*repeating softly*]:
Gray eyes is glass.

BERENICE:
But what I'm warning is this. If you start out falling in love with some unheard-of thing like that, what is going to happen to you? If you take a mania like this, it won't be the last time and of that you can be sure. So what will become of you? Will you be trying to break into weddings the rest of your days?

FRANKIE:
It makes me sick to listen to people who don't have any sense. [*She sticks her fingers in her ears and hums.*]

BERENICE:
You just settin' yourself this fancy trap to catch yourself in trouble. And you know it.

FRANKIE:
They will take me. You wait and see.

BERENICE:
Well, I been trying to reason seriously. But I see it is no use.

FRANKIE:

You are just jealous. You are just trying to deprive me of all the pleasure of leaving town.

BERENICE:

I am just trying to head this off. But I still see it is no use.

JOHN HENRY:

Gray eyes is glass.

[*The piano is played to the seventh note of the scale and this is repeated.*]

FRANKIE [*singing*]:

Do, ray, mee, fa, sol, la, tee, do. Tee. Tee. It could drive you wild. [*She crosses to the screen door and slams it.*] You didn't say anything about Willis Rhodes. Did he have a mashed thumb or a coat or something? [*She returns to the table and sits down.*]

BERENICE:

Lord, now that really was something.

FRANKIE:

I only know he stole your furniture and was so terrible you had to call the Law on him.

BERENICE:

Well, imagine this! Imagine a cold bitter January night. And me laying all by myself in the big parlor bed. Alone in the house because everybody else had gone for the Saturday night. Me, mind you, who hates to sleep in a big empty bed all by myself at any time. Past twelve o'clock on this cold, bitter January night. Can you remember winter time, John Henry? [*John Henry nods.*] Imagine!

81

Suddenly there comes a sloughing sound and a tap, tap, tap. So Miss Me . . . [*She laughs uproariously and stops suddenly, putting her hand over her mouth.*]

FRANKIE:

What? [*leaning closer across the table and looking intently at Berenice*] What happened?

[*Berenice looks from one to the other, shaking her head slowly. Then she speaks in a changed voice.*]

BERENICE:

Why, I wish you would look yonder. I wish you would look. [*Frankie glances quickly behind her, then turns back to Berenice.*]

FRANKIE:

What? What happened?

BERENICE:

Look at them two little pitchers and them four big ears. [*Berenice gets up suddenly from the table.*] Come on, chillin, less us roll out the dough for the cookies tomorrow. [*Berenice clears the table and begins washing dishes at the sink.*]

FRANKIE:

If it's anything I mortally despise, it's a person who starts out to tell something and works up people's interest, and then stops.

BERENICE [*still laughing*]:

I admit it. And I am sorry. But it was just one of them things I suddenly realized I couldn't tell you and John Henry.

[*John Henry skips up to the sink.*]

JOHN HENRY [*singing*]:
Cookies! Cookies! Cookies!

FRANKIE:
You could have sent him out of the room and told me. But don't think I care a particle about what happened. I just wish Willis Rhodes had come in about that time and slit your throat. [*She goes out into the hall.*]

BERENICE [*still chuckling*]:
That is a ugly way to talk. You ought to be ashamed. Here, John Henry, I'll give you a scrap of dough to make a cookie man.

[*Berenice gives John Henry some dough. He climbs up on a chair and begins to work with it. Frankie enters with the evening newspaper. She stands in the doorway, then puts the newspaper on the table.*]

FRANKIE:
I see in the paper where we dropped a new bomb—the biggest one dropped yet. They call it a atom bomb. I intend to take two baths tonight. One long soaking bath and scrub with a brush. I'm going to try to scrape this crust off my elbows. Then let out the dirty water and take a second bath.

BERENICE:
Hooray, that's a good idea. I will be glad to see you clean.

JOHN HENRY:
I will take two baths.

[*Berenice has picked up the paper and is sitting in a chair against the pale white light of the window. She holds the newspaper open before her and her head is twisted down to one side as she strains to see what is printed there.*]

FRANKIE:

Why is it against the law to change your name?

BERENICE:

What is that on your neck? I thought it was a head you carried on that neck. Just think. Suppose I would suddenly up and call myself Mrs. Eleanor Roosevelt. And you would begin naming yourself Joe Louis. And John Henry here tried to pawn himself off as Henry Ford.

FRANKIE:

Don't talk childish; that is not the kind of changing I mean. I mean from a name that doesn't suit you to a name you prefer. Like I changed from Frankie to F. Jasmine.

BERENICE:

But it would be a confusion. Suppose we all suddenly change to entirely different names. Nobody would ever know who anybody was talking about. The whole world would go crazy.

FRANKIE:

I don't see what that has to do with it.

BERENICE:

Because things accumulate around your name. You have a name and one thing after another happens to you and things have accumulated around the name.

FRANKIE:

But what has accumulated around my old name? [*Berenice does not reply.*] Nothing! See! My name just didn't mean anything. Nothing ever happened to me.

BERENICE:

But it will. Things will happen.

FRANKIE:

What?

BERENICE:

You pin me down like that and I can't tell you truthfully. If I could, I wouldn't be sitting here in this kitchen right now, but making a fine living on Wall Street as a wizard. All I can say is that things will happen. Just what, I don't know.

FRANKIE:

Until yesterday, nothing ever happened to me.

[*John Henry crosses to the door and puts on Berenice's hat and shoes, takes her pocketbook and walks around the table twice.*]

BERENICE:

John Henry, take off my hat and my shoes and put up my pocketbook. Thank you very much. [*John Henry does so.*]

FRANKIE:

Listen, Berenice. Doesn't it strike you as strange that I am I and you are you? Like when you are walking down a street and you meet somebody. And you are you. And he

85

is him. Yet when you look at each other, the eyes make a connection. Then you go off one way. And he goes off another way. You go off into different parts of town, and maybe you never see each other again. Not in your whole life. Do you see what I mean?

BERENICE:
Not exactly.

FRANKIE:
That's not what I meant to say anyway. There are all these people here in town I don't even know by sight or name. And we pass alongside each other and don't have any connection. And they don't know me and I don't know them. And now I'm leaving town and there are all these people I will never know.

BERENICE:
But who do you want to know?

FRANKIE:
Everybody. Everybody in the world.

BERENICE:
Why, I wish you would listen to that. How about people like Willis Rhodes? How about them Germans? How about them Japanese?

[Frankie knocks her head against the door jamb and looks up at the ceiling.]

FRANKIE:
That's not what I mean. That's not what I'm talking about.

BERENICE:

Well, what *is* you talking about?

[*A child's voice is heard outside, calling: "Batter up! Batter up!"*]

JOHN HENRY [*in a low voice*]:

Less play out, Frankie.

FRANKIE:

No. You go. [*after a pause*] This is what I mean.

[*Berenice waits, and when Frankie does not speak again, says:*]

BERENICE:

What on earth is wrong with you?

FRANKIE [*after a long pause, then suddenly, with hysteria*]:

Boyoman! Manoboy! When we leave Winter Hill we're going to more places than you ever thought about or even knew existed. Just where we will go first I don't know, and it don't matter. Because after we go to that place we're going on to another. Alaska, China, Iceland, South America. Travelling on trains. Letting her rip on motorcycles. Flying around all over the world in airplanes. Here today and gone tomorrow. All over the world. It's the damn truth. Boyoman! [*She runs around the table.*]

BERENICE:

Frankie!

FRANKIE:

And talking of things happening. Things will happen so fast we won't hardly have time to realize them. Captain

Jarvis Addams wins highest medals and is decorated by the President. Miss F. Jasmine Addams breaks all records. Mrs. Janice Addams elected Miss United Nations in beauty contest. One thing after another happening so fast we don't hardly notice them.

BERENICE:
Hold still, fool.

FRANKIE [*her excitement growing more and more intense*]:
And we will meet them. Everybody. We will just walk up to people and know them right away. We will be walking down a dark road and see a lighted house and knock on the door and strangers will rush to meet us and say: "Come in! Come in!" We will know decorated aviators and New York people and movie stars. We will have thousands and thousands of friends. And we will belong to so many clubs that we can't even keep track of all of them. We will be members of the whole world. Boyoman! Manoboy!

[*Frankie has been running round and round the table in wild excitement and when she passes the next time Berenice catches her slip so quickly that she is caught up with a jerk.*]

BERENICE:
*Is* you gone raving wild? [*She pulls Frankie closer and puts her arm around her waist.*] Sit here in my lap and rest a minute. [*Frankie sits in Berenice's lap. John Henry comes close and jealously pinches Frankie.*] Leave Frankie alone. She ain't bothered you.

JOHN HENRY:
I'm sick.

BERENICE:
Now no, you ain't. Be quiet and don't grudge your cousin
a little bit love.

JOHN HENRY [*hitting Frankie*]:
Old mean bossy Frankie.

BERENICE:
What she doing so mean right now? She just laying here
wore out. [*They continue sitting. Frankie is relaxed now.*]

FRANKIE:
Today I went to the Blue Moon—this place that all the
soldiers are so fond of and I met a soldier—a red-headed
boy.

BERENICE:
What is all this talk about the Blue Moon and soldiers?

FRANKIE:
Berenice, you treat me like a child. When I see all these
soldiers milling around town I always wonder where they
came from and where they are going.

BERENICE:
They were born and they going to die.

FRANKIE:
There are so many things about the world I do not understand.

89

BERENICE:

If you did understand you would be God. Didn't you know that?

FRANKIE:

Maybe so. [*She stares and stretches herself on Berenice's lap, her long legs sprawled out beneath the kitchen table.*] Anyway, after the wedding I won't have to worry about things any more.

BERENICE:

You don't have to now. Nobody requires you to solve the riddles of the world.

FRANKIE [*looking at newspaper*]:

The paper says this new atom bomb is worth twenty thousand tons of T.N.T.

BERENICE:

Twenty thousand tons? And there ain't but two tons of coal in the coal house—all that coal.

FRANKIE:

The paper says the bomb is a very important science discovery.

BERENICE:

The figures these days have got too high for me. Read in the paper about ten million peoples killed. I can't crowd that many peoples in my mind's eye.

JOHN HENRY:

Berenice, is the glass eye your mind's eye?

[*John Henry has climbed up on the back rungs of Berenice's chair and has been hugging her head. He is now holding her ears.*]

BERENICE:

Don't yank my head back like that, Candy. Me and Frankie ain't going to float up through the ceiling and leave you.

FRANKIE:

I wonder if you have ever thought about this? Here we are—right now. This very minute. Now. But while we're talking right now, this minute is passing. And it will never come again. Never in all the world. When it is gone, it is gone. No power on earth could bring it back again.

JOHN HENRY [*beginning to sing*]:

> I sing because I'm happy,
> I sing because I'm free,
> For His eye is on the sparrow,
> And I know He watches me.

BERENICE [*singing*]:

> Why should I feel discouraged?
> Why should the shadows come?
> Why should my heart be lonely,
> Away from heaven and home?
> For Jesus is my portion,
> My constant friend is He,
> For His eye is on the sparrow,
> And I know He watches me.
> So, I sing because I'm happy.

91

[*John Henry and Frankie join on the last three lines.*]

I sing because I'm happy,
I sing because I'm free,
For His eye is on the sparrow,
And I know He watches . . .

BERENICE:

Frankie, you got the sharpest set of human bones I ever felt.

[*The curtain falls.*]

# ACT THREE

## SCENE ONE

*The scene is the same: the kitchen. It is the day of the wed-*
*ding. When the curtain rises Berenice, in her apron, and*
*T. T. Williams in a white coat have just finished prepara-*
*tions for the wedding refreshments. Berenice has been*
*watching the ceremony through the half-open door lead-*
*ing into the hall. There are sounds of congratulations off-*
*stage, the wedding ceremony having just finished.*

||||||||||||||||||||||||||||||||||||||||||||||||||||||||||||||||||||||||||||||||||||||||||||

BERENICE [*to T. T. Williams*]:
Can't see much from this door. But I can see Frankie. And
her face is a study. And John Henry's chewing away at the
bubble gum that Jarvis bought him. Well, sounds like it's
all over. They crowding in now to kiss the bride. We better take this cloth off the sandwiches. Frankie said she
would help you serve.

T. T.:
From the way she's been acting, I don't think we can count
much on her.

BERENICE:
I wish Honey was here. I'm so worried about him since
what you told me. It's going to storm. It's a mercy they
didn't decide to have the wedding in the back yard like
they first planned.

T. T.:
I thought I'd better not minch the matter. Honey was in a
bad way when I saw him this morning.

BERENICE:

Honey Camden don't have too large a share of judgment as it is, but when he gets high on them reefers, he's got no more judgment than a four-year-old child. Remember that time he swung at the police and nearly got his eyes beat out?

T. T.:

Not to mention six months on the road.

BERENICE:

I haven't been so anxious in all my life. I've got two people scouring Sugarville to find him. [in a fervent voice] God, you took Ludie but please watch over my Honey Camden. He's all the family I got.

T. T.:

And Frankie behaving this way about the wedding. Poor little critter.

BERENICE:

And the sorry part is that she's perfectly serious about all this foolishness. [Frankie enters the kitchen through the hall door.] Is it all over? [T. T. crosses to the icebox with sandwiches.]

FRANKIE:

Yes. And it was such a pretty wedding I wanted to cry.

BERENICE:

You told them yet?

FRANKIE:

About my plans—no, I haven't yet told them.

94

[*John Henry comes in and goes out.*]

BERENICE:

Well, you better hurry up and do it, for they going to leave the house right after the refreshments.

FRANKIE:

Oh, I know it. But something just seems to happen to my throat; every time I tried to tell them, different words came out.

BERENICE:
What words?

FRANKIE:

I asked Janice how come she didn't marry with a veil. [*with feeling*] Oh, I'm so embarrassed. Here I am all dressed up in this tacky evening dress. Oh, why didn't I listen to you! I'm so ashamed.

[*T. T. goes out with a platter of sandwiches.*]

BERENICE:
Don't take everything so strenuous like.

FRANKIE:
I'm going in there and tell them now! [*She goes.*]

JOHN HENRY [*coming out of the interior bedroom, carrying several costumes*]:
Frankie sure gave me a lot of presents when she was packing the suitcase. Berenice, she gave me all the beautiful show costumes.

95

BERENICE:

Don't set so much store by all those presents. Come to-morrow morning and she'll be demanding them back again.

JOHN HENRY:

And she even gave me the shell from the Bay. [*He puts the shell to his ear and listens.*]

BERENICE:

I wonder what's going on up there. [*She goes to the door and opens it and looks through.*]

T. T. [*returning to the kitchen*]:

They all complimenting the wedding cake. And drinking the wine punch.

BERENICE:

What's Frankie doing? When she left the kitchen a minute ago she was going to tell them. I wonder how they'll take this total surprise. I have a feeling like you get just before a big thunder storm.

[*Frankie enters, holding a punch cup.*]

BERENICE:

You told them yet?

FRANKIE:

There are all the family around and I can't seem to tell them. I wish I had written it down on the typewriter beforehand. I try to tell them and the words just—die.

BERENICE:

The words just die because the very idea is so silly.

FRANKIE:

I love the two of them so much. Janice put her arms around me and said she had always wanted a little sister. And she kissed me. She asked me again what grade I was in in school. That's the third time she's asked me. In fact, that's the main question I've been asked at the wedding.

[*John Henry comes in, wearing a fairy costume, and goes out. Berenice notices Frankie's punch and takes it from her.*]

FRANKIE:

And Jarvis was out in the street seeing about this car he borrowed for the wedding. And I followed him out and tried to tell him. But while I was trying to reach the point, he suddenly grabbed me by the elbows and lifted me up and sort of swung me. He said: "Frankie, the lankie, the alaga fankie, the tee-legged, toe-legged, bow-legged Frankie." And he gave me a dollar bill.

BERENICE:

That's nice.

FRANKIE:

I just don't know what to do. I have to tell them and yet I don't know how to.

BERENICE:

Maybe when they're settled, they will invite you to come and visit with them.

FRANKIE:

Oh no! I'm going *with* them.

[*Frankie goes back into the house. There are louder sounds of voices from the interior. John Henry comes in again.*]

JOHN HENRY:

The bride and the groom are leaving. Uncle Royal is taking their suitcases out to the car.

[*Frankie runs to the interior room and returns with her suitcase. She kisses Berenice.*]

FRANKIE:

Good-bye, Berenice. Good-bye, John Henry. [*She stands a moment and looks around the kitchen.*] Farewell, old ugly kitchen. [*She runs out.*]

[*There are sounds of good-byes as the wedding party and the family guests move out of the house to the sidewalk. The voices get fainter in the distance. Then, from the front sidewalk there is the sound of disturbance. Frankie's voice is heard, diminished by distance, although she is speaking loudly.*]

FRANKIE'S VOICE:

That's what I am telling you. [*Indistinct protesting voices are heard.*]

MR. ADDAMS' VOICE [*indistinctly*]:

Now be reasonable, Frankie.

FRANKIE'S VOICE [*screaming*]:

I have to go. Take me! Take me!

JOHN HENRY [*entering excitedly*]:

Frankie is in the wedding car and they can't get her out. [*He runs out but soon returns.*] Uncle Royal and my

Daddy are having to haul and drag old Frankie. She's holding onto the steering wheel.

MR. ADDAMS' VOICE:
You march right along here. What in the world has come into you? [*He comes into the kitchen with Frankie who is sobbing.*] I never heard of such an exhibition in my life. Berenice, you take charge of her.

[*Frankie flings herself on the kitchen chair and sobs with her head in her arms on the kitchen table.*]

JOHN HENRY:
They put old Frankie out of the wedding. They hauled her out of the wedding car.

MR. ADDAMS [*clearing his throat*]:
That's sufficient, John Henry. Leave Frankie alone. [*He puts a caressing hand on Frankie's head.*] What makes you want to leave your old papa like this? You've got Janice and Jarvis all upset on their wedding day.

FRANKIE:
I love them so!

BERENICE [*looking down the hall*]:
Here they come. Now please be reasonable, Sugar.

[*The bride and groom come in. Frankie keeps her face buried in her arms and does not look up. The bride wears a blue suit with a white flower corsage pinned at the shoulder.*]

JARVIS:

Frankie, we came to tell you good-bye. I'm sorry you're taking it like this.

JANICE:

Darling, when we are settled we want you to come for a nice visit with us. But we don't yet have any place to live. [*She goes to Frankie and caresses her head. Frankie jerks.*] Won't you tell us good-bye now?

FRANKIE [*with passion*]:

*We!* When you say *we*, you only mean you and Jarvis. And I am not included. [*She buries her head in her arms again and sobs.*]

JANICE:

Please, darling, don't make us unhappy on our wedding day. You know we love you.

FRANKIE:

See! *We*—when you say we, I am not included. It's not fair.

JANICE:

When you come visit us you must write beautiful plays, and we'll all act in them. Come, Frankie, don't hide your sweet face from us. Sit up. [*Frankie raises her head slowly and stares with a look of wonder and misery.*] Good-bye, Frankie, darling.

JARVIS:

So long, now, kiddo.

[*They go out and Frankie still stares at them as they go down the hall. She rises, crosses towards the door and falls on her knees.*]

100

FRANKIE:

Take me! Take me!

[*Berenice puts Frankie back on her chair.*]

JOHN HENRY:

They put Frankie out of the wedding. They hauled her out of the wedding car.

BERENICE:

Don't tease your cousin, John Henry.

FRANKIE:

It was a frame-up all around.

BERENICE:

Well, don't bother no more about it. It's over now. Now cheer up.

FRANKIE:

I wish the whole world would die.

BERENICE:

School will begin now in only three more weeks and you'll find another bosom friend like Evelyn Owen you so wild about.

JOHN HENRY [*seated below the sewing machine*]:

I'm sick, Berenice. My head hurts.

BERENICE:

No you're not. Be quiet, I don't have the patience to fool with you.

FRANKIE [*hugging her hunched shoulders*]:

Oh, my heart feels so cheap!

BERENICE:

Soon as you get started in school and have a chance to make these here friends, I think it would be a good idea to have a party.

FRANKIE:

Those baby promises rasp on my nerves.

BERENICE:

You could call up the society editor of the *Evening Journal* and have the party written up in the paper. And that would make the fourth time your name has been published in the paper.

FRANKIE [*with a trace of interest*]:

When my bike ran into that automobile, the paper called me Fankie Addams, F-A-N-K-I-E. [*She puts her head down again.*]

JOHN HENRY:

Frankie, don't cry. This evening we can put up the teepee and have a good time.

FRANKIE:

Oh, hush up your mouth.

BERENICE:

Listen to me. Tell me what you would like and I will try to do it if it is in my power.

FRANKIE:

All I wish in the world, is for no human being ever to speak to me as long as I live.

BERENICE:

Bawl, then, misery.

[*Mr. Addams enters the kitchen, carrying Frankie's suitcase, which he sets in the middle of the kitchen floor. He cracks his finger joints. Frankie stares at him resentfully, then fastens her gaze on the suitcase.*]

MR. ADDAMS:
Well, it looks like the show is over and the monkey's dead.

FRANKIE:
You think it's over, but it's not.

MR. ADDAMS:
You want to come down and help me at the store to-morrow? Or polish some silver with the shammy rag? You can even play with those old watch springs.

FRANKIE [*still looking at her suitcase*]:
That's my suitcase I packed. If you think it's all over, that only shows how little you know. [*T. T. comes in.*] If I can't go with the bride and my brother as I was meant to leave this town, I'm going anyway. Somehow, anyhow, I'm leaving town. [*Frankie raises up in her chair.*] I can't stand this existence—this kitchen—this town—any longer! I will hop a train and go to New York. Or hitch rides to Hollywood, and get a job there. If worse comes to worse, I can act in comedies. [*She rises.*] Or I could dress up like a boy and join the Merchant Marines and run away to sea. Somehow, anyhow, I'm running away.

BERENICE:
Now quiet down—

FRANKIE [*grabbing the suitcase and running into the hall*]:
Please, Papa, don't try to capture me.

103

[*Outside the wind starts to blow.*]

JOHN HENRY [*from the doorway*]:
Uncle Royal, Frankie's got your pistol in her suitcase.

[*There is the sound of running footsteps and of the screen door slamming.*]

BERENICE:
Run catch her.

[*T. T. and Mr. Addams rush into the hall, followed by John Henry.*]

MR. ADDAMS' VOICE:
Frankie! Frankie! Frankie!

[*Berenice is left alone in the kitchen. Outside the wind is higher and the hall door is blown shut. There is a rumble of thunder, then a loud clap. Thunder and flashes of lightning continue. Berenice is seated in her chair, when John Henry comes in.*]

JOHN HENRY:
Uncle Royal is going with my Daddy, and they are chasing her in our car. [*There is a thunder clap.*] The thunder scares me, Berenice.

BERENICE [*taking him in her lap*]:
Ain't nothing going to hurt you.

JOHN HENRY:
You think they're going to catch her?

BERENICE [*putting her hand to her head*]:
Certainly. They'll be bringing her home directly. I've got such a headache. Maybe my eye socket and all these troubles.

JOHN HENRY [*with his arms around Berenice*]:
I've got a headache, too. I'm sick, Berenice.

BERENICE:
No you ain't. Run along, Candy. I ain't got the patience to fool with you now.

[*Suddenly the lights go out in the kitchen, plunging it in gloom. The sound of wind and storm continues and the yard is a dark storm-green.*]

JOHN HENRY:
Berenice!

BERENICE:
Ain't nothing. Just the lights went out.

JOHN HENRY:
I'm scared.

BERENICE:
Stand still, I'll just light a candle. [*muttering*] I always keep one around, for such like emergencies. [*She opens a drawer.*]

JOHN HENRY:
What makes the lights go out so scarey like this?

BERENICE:
Just one of them things, Candy.

105

JOHN HENRY:
I'm scared. Where's Honey?

BERENICE:
Jesus knows. I'm scared, too. With Honey snow-crazy and loose like this—and Frankie run off with a suitcase and her Papa's pistol. I feel like every nerve been picked out of me.

JOHN HENRY [*holding out his seashell and stroking Berenice*]:
You want to listen to the ocean?

[*The curtain falls.*]

*The scene is the same. There are still signs in the kitchen of the wedding: punch glasses and the punch bowl on the drainboard. It is four o'clock in the morning. As the curtain rises, Berenice and Mr. Addams are alone in the kitchen. There is a crepuscular glow in the yard.*

MR. ADDAMS:

I never was a believer in corporal punishment. Never spanked Frankie in my life, but when I lay my hands on her . . .

BERENICE:

She'll show up soon—but I know how you feel. What with worrying about Honey Camden, John Henry's sickness and Frankie, I've never lived through such a anxious night. [*She looks through the window. It is dawning now.*]

MR. ADDAMS:

I'd better go and find out the last news of John Henry, poor baby. [*He goes through the hall door.*]

[*Frankie comes into the yard and crosses to the arbor. She looks exhausted and almost beaten. Berenice has seen her from the window, rushes into the yard and grabs her by the shoulders and shakes her.*]

BERENICE:

Frankie Addams, you ought to be skinned alive. I been so worried.

FRANKIE:

I've been so worried too.

107

BERENICE:

Where have you been this night? Tell me everything.

FRANKIE:

I will, but quit shaking me.

BERENICE:

Now tell me the A and the Z of this.

FRANKIE:

When I was running around the dark scarey streets, I begun to realize that my plans for Hollywood and the Merchant Marines were child plans that would not work. I hid in the alley behind Papa's store, and it was dark and I was scared. I opened the suitcase and took out Papa's pistol. [*She sits down on her suitcase.*] I vowed I was going to shoot myself. I said I was going to count three and on three pull the trigger. I counted one—two—but I didn't count three—because at the last minute, I changed my mind.

BERENICE:

You march right along with me. You going to bed.

FRANKIE:

Oh, Honey Camden!

[*Honey Camden Brown, who has been hiding behind the arbor, has suddenly appeared.*]

BERENICE:

Oh, Honey, Honey. [*They embrace.*]

HONEY:

Shush, don't make any noise; the law is after me.

108

BERENICE [*in a whisper*]:
Tell me.

HONEY:
Mr. Wilson wouldn't serve me so I drew a razor on him.

BERENICE:
You kill him?

HONEY:
Didn't have no time to find out. I been runnin' all night.

FRANKIE:
Lightfoot, if you drew a razor on a white man, you'd better not let them catch you.

BERENICE:
Here's six dolla's. If you can get to Fork Falls and then to Atlanta. But be careful slippin' through the white folks' section. They'll be combing the county looking for you.

HONEY [*with passion*]:
Don't cry, Berenice.

BERENICE:
Already I feel that rope.

HONEY:
Don't you dare cry. I know now all my days have been leading up to this minute. No more "boy this—boy that" —no bowing, no scraping. For the first time, I'm free and it makes me happy. [*He begins to laugh hysterically.*]

BERENICE:
When they catch you, they'll string you up.

HONEY [*beside himself, brutally*]:
Let them hang me—I don't care. I tell you I'm glad. I tell you I'm happy. [*He goes out behind the arbor.*]

FRANKIE [*calling after him*]:
Honey, remember you are Lightfoot. Nothing can stop you if you want to run away.

[*Mrs. West, John Henry's mother, comes into the yard.*]

MRS. WEST:
What was all that racket? John Henry is critically ill. He's got to have perfect quiet.

FRANKIE:
John Henry's sick, Aunt Pet?

MRS. WEST:
The doctors say he has meningitis. He must have perfect quiet.

BERENICE:
I haven't had time to tell you yet. John Henry took sick sudden last night. Yesterday afternoon when I complained of my head, he said he had a headache too and thinking he copies me I said, "Run along, I don't have the patience to fool with you." Looks like a judgment on me. There won't be no more noise, Mrs. West.

MRS. WEST:
Make sure of that. [*She goes away.*]

FRANKIE [*putting her arm around Berenice*]:
Oh, Berenice, what can we do?

110

BERENICE [*stroking Frankie's head*]:
Ain't nothing we can do but wait.

FRANKIE:
The wedding—Honey—John Henry—so much has happened that my brain can't hardly gather it in. Now for the first time I realize that the world is certainly—a sudden place.

BERENICE:
Sometimes sudden, but when you are waiting, like this, it seems so slow.

[*The curtain falls.*]

*The scene is the same: the kitchen and arbor. It is months later, a November day, about sunset.*

*The arbor is brittle and withered. The elm tree is bare except for a few ragged leaves. The yard is tidy and the lemonade stand and sheet stage curtain are now missing. The kitchen is neat and bare and the furniture has been removed. Berenice, wearing a fox fur, is sitting in a chair with an old suitcase and doll at her feet. Frankie enters.*

FRANKIE:

Oh, I am just mad about these Old Masters.

BERENICE:

Humph!

FRANKIE:

The house seems so hollow. Now that the furniture is packed. It gives me a creepy feeling in the front. That's why I came back here.

BERENICE:

Is that the only reason why you came back here?

FRANKIE:

Oh, Berenice, you know. I wish you hadn't given quit notice just because Papa and I are moving into a new house with Uncle Eustace and Aunt Pet out in Limewood.

BERENICE:

I respect and admire Mrs. West but I'd never get used to working for her.

FRANKIE:

Mary is just beginning this Rachmaninoff Concerto. She may play it for her debut when she is eighteen years old. Mary playing the piano and the whole orchestra playing at one and the same time, mind you. Awfully hard.

BERENICE:

Ma-ry Littlejohn.

FRANKIE:

I don't know why you always have to speak her name in a tinged voice like that.

BERENICE:

Have I ever said anything against her? All I said was that she is too lumpy and marshmallow white and it makes me nervous to see her just setting there sucking them pigtails.

FRANKIE:

Braids. Furthermore, it is no use our discussing a certain party. You could never possibly understand it. It's just not in you.

[*Berenice looks at her sadly, with faded stillness, then pats and strokes the fox fur.*]

BERENICE:

Be that as it may. Less us not fuss and quarrel this last afternoon.

FRANKIE:

I don't want to fuss either. Anyway, this is not our last afternoon. I will come and see you often.

113

BERENICE:

No, you won't, baby. You'll have other things to do. Your road is already strange to me.

[*Frankie goes to Berenice, pats her on the shoulder, then takes her fox fur and examines it.*]

FRANKIE:

You still have the fox fur that Ludie gave you. Somehow this little fur looks so sad—so thin and with a sad little fox-wise face.

BERENICE [*taking the fur back and continuing to stroke it*]:

Got every reason to be sad. With what has happened in these two last months. I just don't know what I have done to deserve it. [*She sits, the fur in her lap, bent over with her forearms on her knees and her hands limply dangling.*] Honey gone and John Henry, my little boy gone.

FRANKIE:

You did all you could. You got poor Honey's body and gave him a Christian funeral and nursed John Henry.

BERENICE:

It's the way Honey died and the fact that John Henry had to suffer so. Little soul!

FRANKIE:

It's peculiar—the way it all happened so fast. First Honey caught and hanging himself in the jail. Then later in that same week, John Henry died and then I met Mary. As the irony of fate would have it, we first got to know each other in front of the lipstick and cosmetics counter at Woolworth's. And it was the week of the fair.

BERENICE:

The most beautiful September I ever seen. Countless white and yellow butterflies flying around them autumn flowers—Honey dead and John Henry suffering like he did and daisies, golden weather, butterflies—such strange death weather.

FRANKIE:

I never believed John Henry would die. [*There is a long pause. She looks out the window.*] Don't it seem quiet to you in here? [*There is another, longer pause.*] When I was a little child I believed that out under the arbor at night there would come three ghosts and one of the ghosts wore a silver ring. [*whispering*] Occasionally when it gets so quiet like this I have a strange feeling. It's like John Henry is hovering somewhere in this kitchen—solemn looking and ghost-grey.

A BOY'S VOICE [*from the neighboring yard*]:
Frankie, Frankie.

FRANKIE [*calling to the boy*]:
Yes, Barney. [*to Berenice*] Clock stopped. [*She shakes the clock.*]

THE BOY'S VOICE:
Is Mary there?

FRANKIE [*to Berenice*]:
It's Barney MacKean. [*to the boy, in a sweet voice*] Not yet. I'm meeting her at five. Come on in, Barney, won't you?

115

BARNEY:
Just a minute.

FRANKIE [*to Berenice*]:
Barney puts me in mind of a Greek god.

BERENICE:
What? Barney puts you in mind of a what?

FRANKIE:
Of a Greek god. Mary remarked that Barney reminded her of a Greek god.

BERENICE:
It looks like I can't understand a thing you say no more.

FRANKIE:
You know, those old-timey Greeks worship those Greek gods.

BERENICE:
But what has that got to do with Barney MacKean?

FRANKIE:
On account of the figure.

[*Barney MacKean, a boy of thirteen, wearing a football suit, bright sweater and cleated shoes, runs up the back steps into the kitchen.*]

BERENICE:
Hi, Greek god Barney. This afternoon I saw your initials chalked down on the front sidewalk. M.L. loves B.M.

116

BARNEY:

If I could find out who wrote it, I would rub it out with their faces. Did you do it, Frankie?

FRANKIE [*drawing herself up with sudden dignity*]:
I wouldn't do a kid thing like that. I even resent you asking me. [*She repeats the phrase to herself in a pleased undertone.*] Resent you asking me.

BARNEY:

Mary can't stand me anyhow.

FRANKIE:

Yes she can stand you. I am her most intimate friend. I ought to know. As a matter of fact she's told me several lovely compliments about you. Mary and I are riding on the moving van to our new house. Would you like to go?

BARNEY:

Sure.

FRANKIE:

O.K. You will have to ride back with the furniture 'cause Mary and I are riding on the front seat with the driver. We had a letter from Jarvis and Janice this afternoon. Jarvis is with the Occupation Forces in Germany and they took a vacation trip to Luxembourg. [*She repeats in a pleased voice:*] Luxembourg. Berenice, don't you think that's a lovely name?

BERENICE:

It's kind of a pretty name, but it reminds me of soapy water.

117

FRANKIE:

Mary and I will most likely pass through Luxembourg when we—are going around the world together.

[*Frankie goes out followed by Barney and Berenice sits in the kitchen alone and motionless. She picks up the doll, looks at it and hums the first two lines of "I Sing Because I'm Happy." In the next house the piano is heard again, as the curtain falls.*]

# Playwrights and their plays

**PUBLISHED BY NEW DIRECTIONS**

Wolfgang Borchert
*The Man Outside*

Mikhail Bulgakov
*Flight & Bliss*

Jean Cocteau
*The Infernal Machine & Other Plays*

H.D.
*Ion* and *Hippolytus Temporizes*

Lawrence Ferlinghetti
*Routines* (experimental plays)

Goethe
*Faust,* Part I

Alfred Jarry
*Ubu Roi*

Heinrich von Kleist
*Prince Friedrich of Homburg*

P. Lal
*Great Sanskrit Plays in Modern Translation*

Federico García Lorca
*Five Plays: Comedies and Tragicomedies*
*The Public* and *Play Without a Title*
*Three Tragedies:*
        *The House of Bernard Alba*
        *Blood Wedding*
        *Yerma*

Abby Mann
*Judgment at Nuremberg*

Michael McClure
  *Gorf*

Carson McCullers
  *The Member of the Wedding,*
    Introduction by Dorothy Allison

Henry Miller
  *Just Wild About Harry*

Ezra Pound
  *The Classic Noh Theatre of Japan*
  *Elektra*
  *Women of Trachis*

Kenneth Rexroth
  *Beyond the Mountains* (four plays in verse)

Andrew Sinclair
  *Adventures in the Skin Trade*
    (based on the novel by Dylan Thomas)

Dylan Thomas
  *The Doctor and the Devils* (film and radio scripts)
  *Under Milk Wood*

Tennessee Williams
  *Baby Doll & Tiger Tail*
  *Battle of Angels*
  *Camino Real*
  *Candles to the Sun*
  *Cat on a Hot Tin Roof,*
    Introduction by Edward Albee
  *Clothes for a Summer Hotel*
  *Dragon Country* (short plays)
  *The Eccentricities of a Nightingale*
  *Fugitive Kind*
  *The Glass Menagerie*

PLEASE VISIT OUR WEBSITE
www.ndpublishing.com
OR ORDER FROM YOUR LOCAL BOOKSTORE